United States
Department of
Agriculture

Forest Service

Southern
Research Station

Resource Bulletin
SRS–143

Alabama's Forests, 2000

Andrew J. Hartsell and
Tony G. Johnson

Streams, such as this one in Colbert County, play an important role in ecosystem health. (photo by Kelvin J. Daniels)

March 2009

Southern Research Station
200 W.T. Weaver Blvd.
Asheville, NC 28804

Alabama's Forests, 2000

Andrew J. Hartsell, Research Forester,
Forest Inventory and Analysis,
Knoxville, TN

Tony G. Johnson, Resource Analyst,
Forest Inventory and Analysis
Knoxville, TN

Foreword

This resource bulletin highlights the principal findings of the seventh forest survey of Alabama. Field work began in May 1997 and was completed in April 2000. Six previous surveys, completed in 1936, 1953, 1963, 1972, 1982, and 1990, provide statistics for measuring changes and trends over the past 64 years. This report primarily emphasizes changes and trends since 1990 and discusses the extent and condition of forest land, associated timber volumes, and rates of timber growth, and removals.

Periodic surveys of our Nation's forest resources are mandated by the Forest and Rangeland Renewable Resources Research Act of 1978. These surveys are a continuing, nationwide undertaking by the regional experiment stations of the Forest Service, U.S. Department of Agriculture (Smith and others 2004). Inventories of the 13 Southern States (Alabama, Arkansas, Florida, Georgia, Kentucky, Louisiana, Mississippi, North Carolina, Oklahoma, South Carolina, Tennessee, Texas, and Virginia) and the Commonwealth of Puerto Rico are conducted by the Southern Research Station (SRS) Forest Inventory and Analysis (FIA) Research Work Unit, operating from its headquarters in Knoxville, TN, and offices in Asheville, NC, and Starkville, MS. The primary objective of these periodic appraisals is to develop and maintain the resource information needed to formulate sound forest policies and programs as mandated by the Agricultural Research Extension and Education Reform Act of 1998 (Farm Bill). More information is available about Forest Service resource inventories (U.S. Department of Agriculture Forest Service 1992) on the Web at http://fia.fs.fed.us/.

Data included in FIA reports are designed to provide a comprehensive array of forest resource statistics, but additional data can be obtained for those who require more specialized information. The forest resource data for Southern States can be accessed directly via the Internet at http://srsfia2.fs.fed.us. FIA data also are available for tabular and mapping output at http://ncrs2.fs.fed.us/4801/fiadb/.

Information concerning any aspect of this survey may be obtained from:

U.S. Department of Agriculture
Forest Service
Southern Research Station
Forest Inventory and Analysis
4700 Old Kingston Pike
Knoxville, TN 37919
Phone: 865-862-2000

Acknowledgments

The SRS gratefully acknowledges the cooperation and excellent assistance provided by the Alabama Forestry Commission in the collection of field data. Production of this bulletin was made possible by the collaboration of many FIA personnel (including those in Data Collection, Data Compilation, Analysis, and Publication Management). We also appreciate the cooperation of other public agencies and private landowners in providing access to measurement plots.

Contents

Highlights from the Seventh Inventory of Alabama

Area

- Alabama's boundaries encompass 32.5 million acres. Of that total, 23 million acres were classified as forest land. Forest land classified as timberland totaled 22.9 million acres, up 4.5 percent, or 1.0 million acres, since 1990.

- Nonindustrial private forest (NIPF) ownership increased 12 percent to 18.0 million acres. Corporate ownership, which constitutes this grouping, increased 41 percent to 2.6 million acres; ownership by individuals increased 9 percent to 15.4 million acres. NIPF owners control 78 percent of Alabama's timberland.

- Forest stands classified as hardwood forest types accounted for 46 percent of the timberland area, an increase of 7 percent since 1990.

- The area of softwood stands rose 9 percent to 8.1 million acres, or 35 percent of the timberland area. Loblolly pine stands experienced a 21 percent increase during this time and accounted for 6.4 million acres of timberland across the State.

- Planted stands accounted for 24 percent of the timberland area in 2000 compared to 18 percent in 1990.

- The area of mixed pine-hardwood stands decreased 7 percent to 4.2 million acres.

Volume

- Softwood all-live volume increased 17 percent to 13.3 billion cubic feet between 1990 and 2000. Most of this increase occurred on NIPF lands, as softwood growing stock on these lands increased by 31 percent to 9.7 billion cubic feet.

- Loblolly pine remained the single most abundant softwood species. At almost 9 billion cubic feet, the species accounted for 68 percent of the 2000 live softwood inventory. Growing-stock volume of softwoods in planted loblolly-shortleaf pine stands increased 105 percent to 3.8 billion cubic feet over the 10-year period between surveys.

- Volume of live hardwoods increased 17 percent to 17.9 billion cubic feet. Eighty-three percent of live hardwood volume was on NIPF lands, 9 percent occurred on lands controlled by forest industry, and the remaining 8 percent was on lands owned by public agencies. Other red oaks was the predominate species group with 4.0 billion cubic feet.

Net Growth and Removals

- Net annual growth of all-live softwoods averaged 923 million cubic feet, an increase of 42 percent since 1990.

- Softwood growth increased in all ownership classes: It was up 45 percent to 612 million cubic feet on NIPF land, 29 percent to 269 million cubic feet on industry lands, 76 percent to 24 million cubic feet on national forest holdings, and 118 percent to 17 million cubic feet on public lands.

- Annual removals of live softwoods averaged 914 million cubic feet, up 26 percent since the previous survey period. Planted stands accounted for 30 percent of the softwood removals.

- Net annual growth of all-live hardwoods averaged 690 million cubic feet, an increase of 23 percent since the 1990 survey.

- Annual removals of hardwood growing stock averaged 465 million cubic feet, up 19 percent since 1990.

Timber Product Output

- Alabama's forest products industry contributed more than $12 billion annually to the State's economy during this survey period.

- The manufacture of forest products accounted for 18 percent of the State's total manufacturing.

- Alabama's forests produced 782 million cubic feet of pulpwood and 429 million cubic feet of saw-log volume per year.

Stand Structure

- The number of hardwood trees per acre increased for each diameter class except the 4-inch class.

- Since the 1990 survey, the number of softwood trees per acre has increased for each diameter class.

- Statewide, all-live basal area on timberland averaged 82.4 square feet per acre. Softwood basal area averaged 32.3 square feet per acre, and hardwood basal area averaged 50.1 square feet per acre.

- Since 1990, average basal area per acre increased 15 percent for softwoods and 9.5 percent for hardwoods.

- In 1972, 66 percent of Alabama's timberland was classified as either poorly stocked or optimally stocked. Today, 76 percent of the State's timberland resources are classified as either fully stocked or overstocked.

Plantations

- Planted stands account for 34 percent of Alabama's softwood volume, 52 percent of the softwood growth, and 47 percent of the State's softwood removals annually.

- Plantations are composed primarily of loblolly pine, as 82 percent of the all-live volume found in these forests is composed of this one species.

- Forests derived from artificial regeneration produce more all-live volume per acre than natural stands.

- Natural stands tend to have a greater variety of species, especially hardwoods, and have larger diameter distributions.

Forests help protect streams and rivers. (photo by Andrew J. Hartsell)

Forest Area/Land-Use Status Trends

Alabama's boundaries encompass 32.5 million acres of land area. Forests comprised 23 million acres or 70.8 percent of the total land area. Forest area classified as timberland totaled 22.9 million acres. Most of this report's discussions will refer to timberland area when making forest area comparisons. The remaining 0.1 million acres of forest land are categorized as reserved timberland, such as wilderness, parks, and historic sites, where commercial timber harvesting is prohibited by statute or administrative regulation. Only 2,800 acres of Alabama's forest area are classified as other forest land. Other forest acreage generally consisted of forest areas incapable of commercial timber production because of adverse site conditions, e.g., rock outcrops, dry and infertile areas, poorly drained pocosins, and harsh coastal environments.

The State's diverse physical characteristics and weather patterns basically have defined the ecology of Alabama's forests. The most notable physiographic feature of the State is the Fall Line that separates the Coastal Plain regions from the Limestone Plateau (Highland Rim), Cumberland Mountain Plateau, Great Appalachian Valley (Coosa Valley), Blue Ridge-Talladega Mountain, and Piedmont regions (Hodgkins and others 1976). In the regions north of the Fall Line, elevations range from 1,000 feet to 2,400 feet above sea level (at Cheaha Mountain). Alabama's Coastal Plain lies below the Fall Line. The Coastal Plain is divided into the Hilly Coastal Plain, Middle Coastal Plain, and Flatlands Coastal Plain. The Black Belt Prairie is an east-west section that runs through the middle of the Hilly Coastal Plain.

Alabama lies almost wholly within the warm-temperate zone. The southern tips of Baldwin and Mobile Counties are classified as subtropical. The length of frost-free periods, i.e., the growing season, averages 8 months. The growing season is 1 month longer in the southern part of the State (Zahner 1984).

Alabama was divided into six survey units when the initial inventory of the State was performed in 1936 (fig. 1). At

Figure 1—Forest survey regions in Alabama.

that time, Alabama's timberland covered 18.9 million acres (fig. 2). Eighty-four percent of those forests were classified as second growth (table 1). Roughly one-half of the second-growth timberland was estimated to be of saw-log size (based on different criteria than current standards). Only 2.5 million acres of "old-growth" acreage was left.

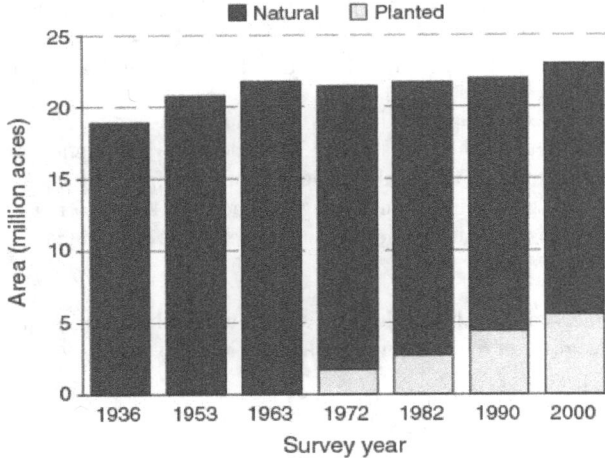

Figure 2—Area of timberland by stand origin and survey year, Alabama.

Table 1—Area of timberland classified according to forest condition, Alabama, 1936[a]

Forest condition	Area	Proportion
	thousand acres	*percent*
Old growth		
Uncut	783.7	4
Partial cut	1,713.9	9
Total	2,497.6	13
Second growth		
Saw-log size		
Uncut	5,034.9	27
Partial cut	2,641.3	14
Under saw-log size	7,336.9	39
Reproduction	864.3	5
Total	15,877.4	84
Clearcut	485.4	3
Total	18,860.4	100

Numbers in columns may not sum to totals due to rounding.
[a] McWilliams (1992).

The second survey (1951 to 1953) showed a total timberland area increase of 10 percent (Wheeler 1953). Abandonment of agriculture land was cited as the primary source of this new timberland. Poletimber stands occupied over one-half of the timberland area, while overall stocking had increased.

The 1963 survey revealed that timberland area continued to increase (Sternitzke 1963). Natural seeding following farmland abandonment and planting of idle cropland under the Federal Soil Bank Program were the primary contributors to the 4.8 percent increase in timberland since 1953. In all, from 1936 to 1963, timberland area increased 15 percent, or 2.8 million acres.

The first decrease in Alabama's timberland was reported in the 1972 survey. Agricultural uses were reclaiming timberland, mainly for use as pastures. Total timberland area for the State was then 21.3 million acres. The 1982 and 1990 forest inventories reported 1.4 percent and 1.3 percent increases in timberland area, respectively.

Today, forests cover 23 million acres or over two-thirds of the total land area of Alabama. A small area, 61,900 acres, has been withdrawn from timber utilization. An additional 2,800 acres, in Baldwin County, are considered incapable of commercial timber production. This acreage, composed of marshland fringes on the southern tip of the county, never had been inventoried.

Plantation forestry has played an important role in the shaping of Alabama's forest resources. Plantations were first recorded by the forest survey in 1972. Since then, the area of plantations has increased 225 percent. In fact, artificially regenerated stands now cover 5.5 million acres, or almost one-quarter of the State's timberland.

Land-Use Change

In Alabama between 1990 and 2000, the area added to timberland exceeded the amount of timberland lost to land clearing (table 2). The area added to timberland totaled 1.7 million acres. Sixty-three percent of the added area was in the Southeast and North Central survey units. The largest increase in added timberland has been in the Southeast survey unit, where timberland additions increased 8 percent to 6.4 million acres. Seventy-seven percent of all forest additions, on an area basis, resulted in conversions from agricultural land.

Altogether, the diversion of timberland to another land use removed 702,600 acres from the timberland base. Diversions to urban or other nonagricultural uses totaled 467,500 acres or 66.5 percent of total diversions. This category includes

Table 2—Change in area of Alabama's timberland between 1990 and 2000, by survey unit

Survey unit	Timber-land	Change	Additions			Diversions		
			Total	Agri-culture	Other	Total	Agri-culture	Other
					thousand acres			
Southwest-South	2,778.0	37.1	96.7	80.6	16.1	-59.7	-10.9	-48.8
Southwest-North	3,599.4	136.0	170.1	148.2	22.0	-34.2	-28.5	-5.7
Southeast	6,373.6	454.6	624.1	506.6	117.6	-169.6	-70.2	-99.4
West-Central	3,404.2	46.8	131.3	101.0	30.3	-84.5	-11.3	-73.3
North-Central	4,524.6	178.6	437.9	306.6	131.4	-259.4	-74.9	-178.7
North	2,246.0	140.9	236.1	167.0	69.1	-95.2	-28.0	-61.6
Total	22,925.8	993.8	1,696.4	1,309.9	386.5	-702.6	-223.7	-467.5

Numbers in rows and colums may not sum to totals due to rounding.

residential and industrial development, roads and highways, utility rights-of-ways, reservoir creation, and many other uses that are usually permanent in nature. This type of forest clearing was most prevalent in the North Central unit. Forest clearing for agricultural purposes claimed another 223,700 acres of timberland area.

The Southeast unit had the largest net gain in timberland. The increase there accounted for almost one-half (46 percent) of the State's 993,800-acre gain in timberland. The state-wide increase represents the largest increase in the State's timberland area since the 1963 forest inventory.

Many counties in the Black Belt Prairie experienced losses in timberland area, especially Winston County. Winston County was the only county to lose > 5 percent of its timberland resource since the 1990 survey period.

The largest gain in timberland area occurred in Houston County which increased its timberland by 33 percent. Large increases in timberland area also occurred in Etowah, Lauderdale, and Limestone Counties since 1990 (fig. 3).

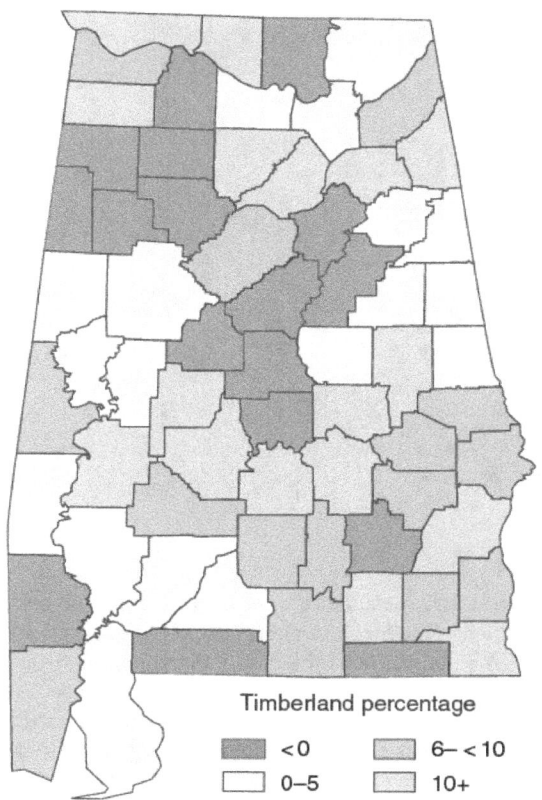

Figure 3—Percent change in timberland by county, Alabama, 1990 to 2000.

Alabama Forestry Commission fire crew at work. (photo courtesy of the Alabama Forestry Commission)

Ownership

The area of timberland in nonindustrial private forest (NIPF) ownership increased 17 percent after 1990 (fig. 4), due in large measure to the fact that forest industry divested itself of much of its holdings in that decade. The NIPF ownership category comprises three distinct groups: (1) farm owners, (2) corporate owners, and (3) individuals. Collectively, these entities controlled 78 percent of Alabama's timberland area. During the same timeframe, timberlands owned by forest industries decreased 32 percent to 3.7 million acres. This is in stark contrast with prior forest inventories. Up until 1990, total NIPF timberland ownership had decreased, while timberland controlled by forest industry had increased. Timberlands owned by the National Forest System have remained fairly consistent for almost one-half century. Since 1972, timberland under the control of other public agencies has gradually increased. Other public acreage increased 12 percent from 1990 to 2000.

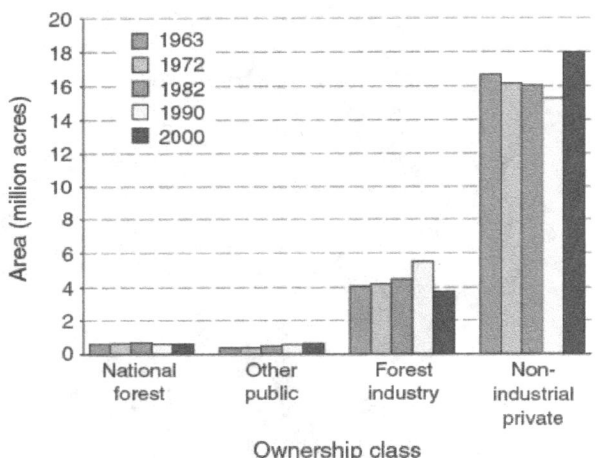

Figure 4—Area of timberland by ownership class and survey year, Alabama.

Forest Type

The forest survey recognized six major forest-type groups in Alabama—the longleaf-slash pine, loblolly-shortleaf pine, oak-pine, oak-hickory, oak-gum-cypress, and elm-ash-cottonwood. These groupings facilitate analysis and representation of data but may mask some important changes or trends in resources. Some changes would not show up in analyses at the level of the forest-type group, whereas more detailed typing would reveal these trends. For example, a shift from longleaf to slash plantings would require specificity lacking in the broader forest-type grouping. Which is to say, because both species are in the

Alabama's forests provide important habitat to many wildlife species such as this squirrel. (photo by Andrew J. Hartsell)

same forest-type group, a replacement of one by the other would go undetected, because the total area in the forest-type group would remain the same.

The predominant forest-type group in Alabama was oak-hickory (occupying 33 percent of all timberland), followed closely by loblolly-shortleaf pine (31 percent) (fig. 5). Oak-pine (18 percent) ranked third, followed by oak-gum-cypress (12 percent). Longleaf-slash pine, at <5 percent, was a distant fifth.

The six forest-type groups can be further classified on the basis of stand origin, i.e., on the basis that they were regenerated by natural or artificial methods. All forest-type groups except oak-gum-cypress and elm-ash-cottonwood are classified by stand origin to derive forest management types.

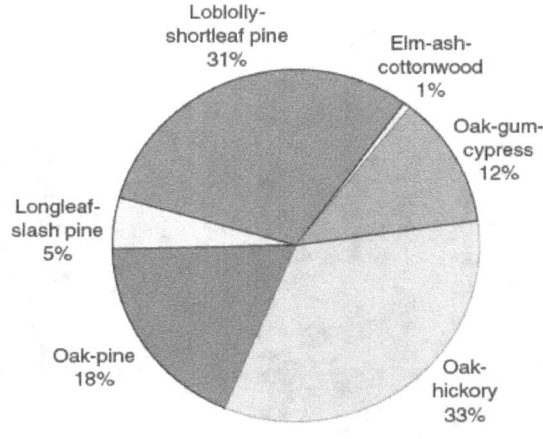

22.9 million acres

Figure 5—Proportion of timberland by forest-type group, Alabama, 2000.

Since 1963, Alabama's forests have undergone considerable changes in species composition, forest-cover types, and stand origin (fig. 6) (stand origin data was not collected in 1963). The biggest change has occurred between planted and natural, loblolly-shortleaf pine stands. The area of natural loblolly-shortleaf pine stands decreased 51 percent between 1972 and 2000. At the same time, the area of planted loblolly-shortleaf pine stands increased 422 percent. These changes are even more dramatic if 1963 estimates, which do not differentiate between planted and natural stands, are included.

For two of the three softwood forest-type groups (loblolly-shortleaf pine and oak-pine), natural stand area decreased as planted stand area increased. Natural and planted longleaf-slash pine both decreased by 29 percent in area after 1972. The acreage in natural oak-pine stands decreased 33 percent, while that in planted stands increased 239 percent. The area of hardwood stands has increased since 1963. Oak-hickory, oak-gum-cypress, and elm-ash-cottonwood have alll experienced increases. It should be noted that the magnitude of some of these increases occurred because these forest-type groups occupied a relatively small portion of timberland area, and any percent change will look significant.

A waterfall in Colbert County. (photo by Kelvin J. Daniels)

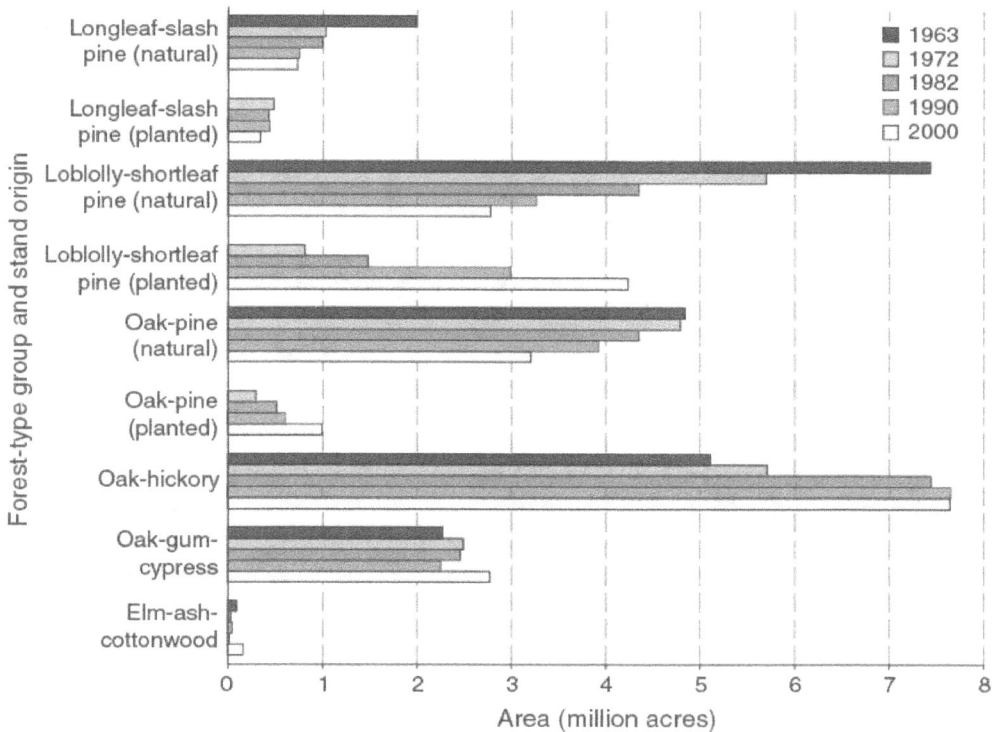

Figure 6—Area of timberland by forest-type group, stand origin, and survey year, Alabama.

Status and Trends of Current Inventory Volume

Softwood Inventory

Volume of softwood growing stock on timberland in Alabama increased 1.6 billion cubic feet between 1990 and 2000 (fig. 7). This increase contrasts with the previous survey in which softwood volume decreased. Softwood growing-stock volume for the State has increased 125 percent over the last one-half of the century, increasing from 5.6 billion in cubic feet in 1956 to 12.6 billion cubic feet today. Growing stock is the measure used in comparing tree volumes over time, as it was the standard used in the original surveys. FIA currently emphasizes all-live volume in assessing forest health and condition, as it considers the entire biologic resource, and not an arbitrary definition based on utilization. The following analysis is based on all-live volumes.

Most of the softwood volume increase occurred on NIPF land, where live softwood volume increased from 7.4 billion cubic feet in 1990 to 9.7 billion cubic feet in 2000, an

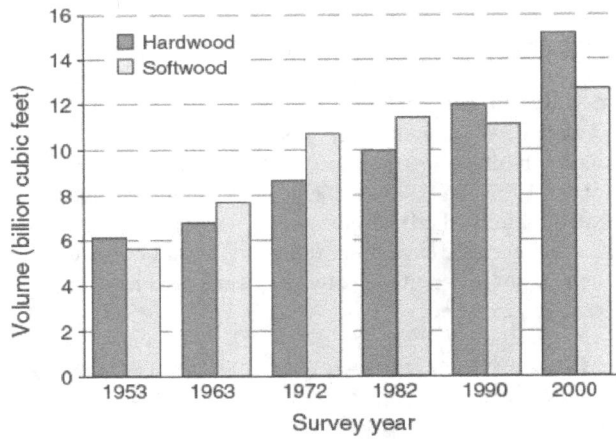

Figure 7—Volume of growing stock on timberland by species group and survey year, Alabama.

A well stocked softwood plantation in Escambia County, Alabama, T.R. Miller Company, November 1963. (photo by William D. Boyer, USDA Forest Service, Bugwood.org)

increase of 31 percent (fig. 8). Some of the increase in volume on NIPF lands can be attributed to the decrease in volume on industry lands. Softwood volume on timberlands controlled by forest industry declined 20 percent to 2.4 billion cubic feet. Volume on national forest lands has remained fairly constant since 1972. On timberland held by other public agencies, volume of live softwoods increased from 0.27 billion cubic feet to 0.47 billion cubic feet (71 percent).

The majority of the 1990 to 2000 increase in softwood volume inventory occurred in planted stands, particularly loblolly-shortleaf pine (fig. 9). All-live volume of softwoods in planted loblolly-shortleaf pine stands increased 105 percent to 3.8 billion cubic feet over the 10-year period. All other forest types, except natural longleaf-slash pine and planted-oak stands, experienced a decrease in softwood volume.

Softwood volume has risen in all survey units across the State (fig. 10). The general trend since 1972 is that softwood volume has gradually increased in almost all units. There was a small decrease in the Southwest unit [fig. 10 (SW)] in 1982 and larger decreases in the West Central [fig. 10 (WC)] and North Central [fig. 10 (NC)] units in the 1990 survey.

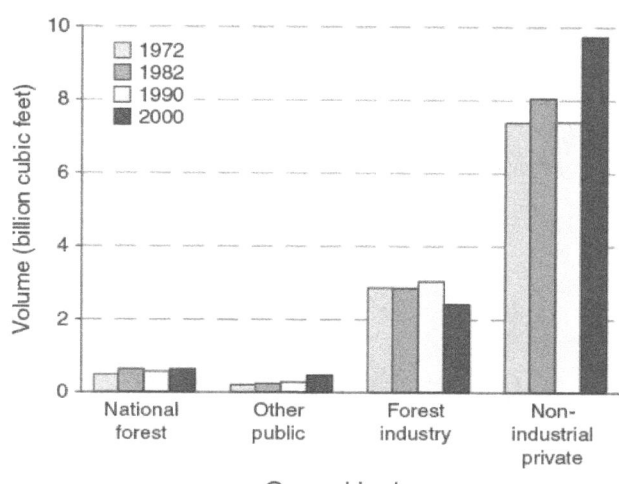

Figure 8—Volume of live softwoods on timberland by ownership class and survey year, Alabama.

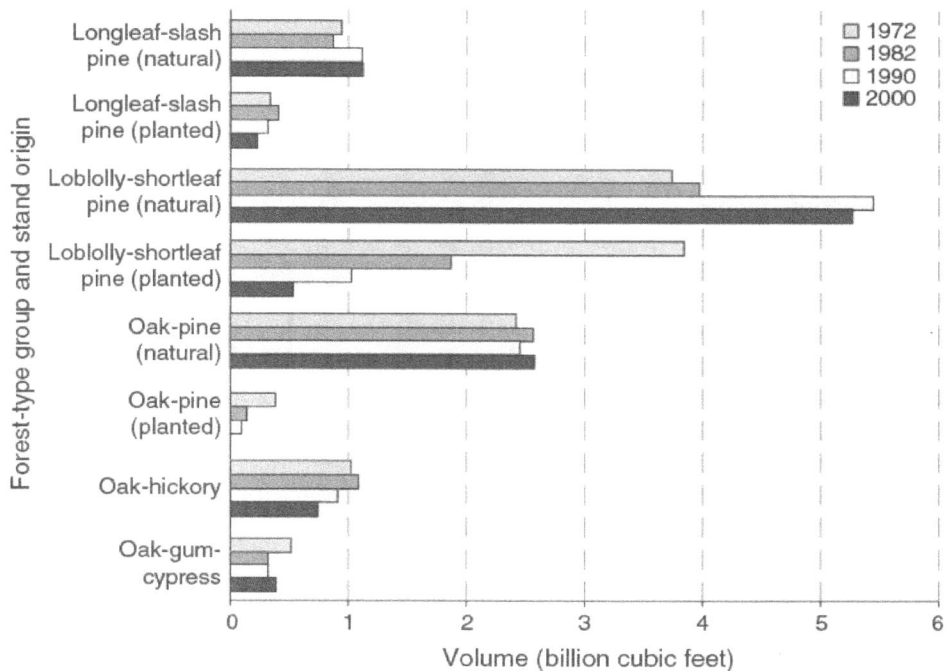

Figure 9—Volume of live softwoods on timberland by forest-type group, stand origin, and survey year, Alabama.

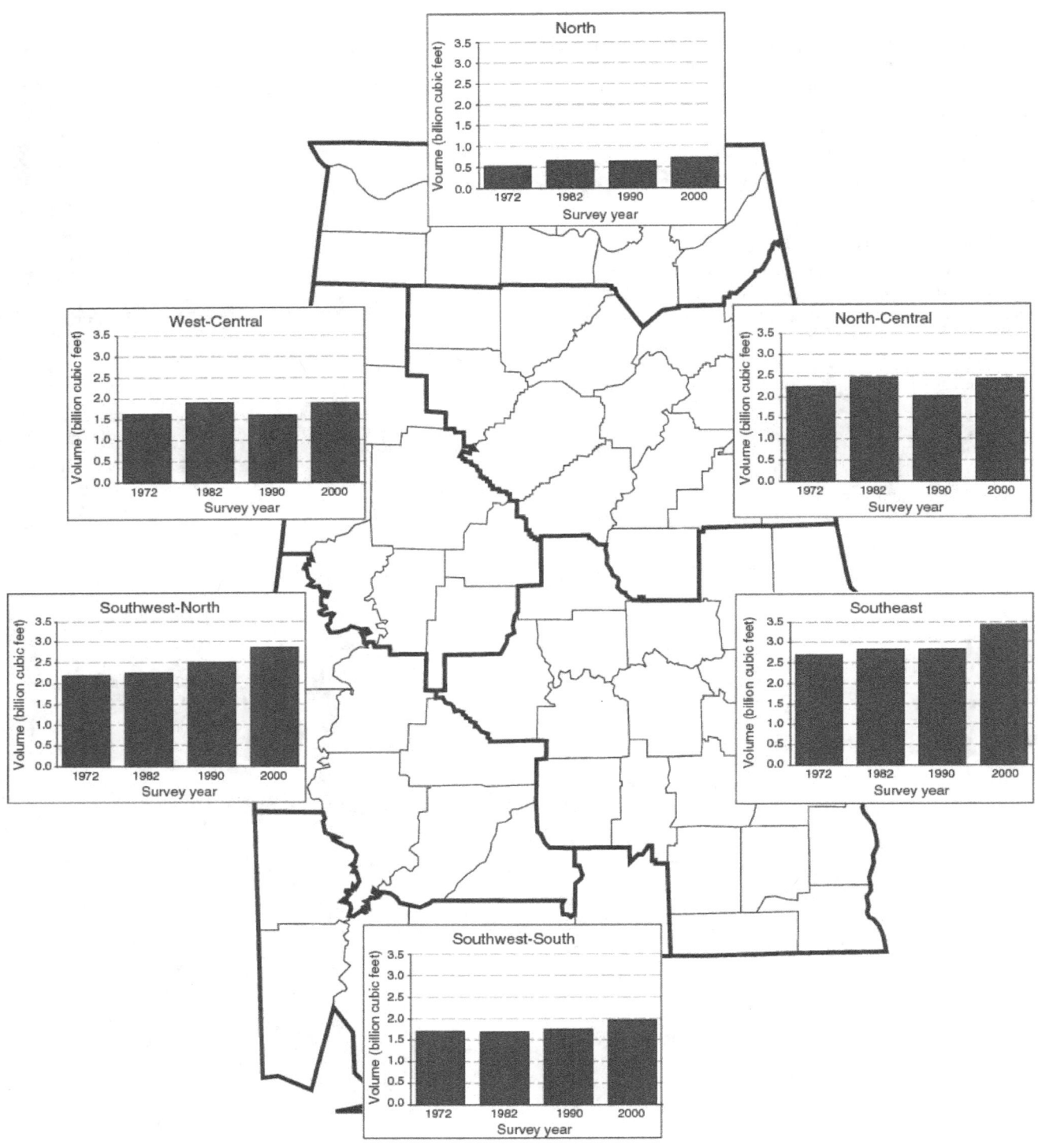

Figure 10—Volume of live softwood on timberland by survey unit for four inventory cycles, Alabama.

The 2000 softwood inventories by unit are higher than those reported in 1972. Increases in softwood volume between 1972 and 2000 ranged from 8 percent in the North Central unit to 37 percent in the North [fig. 10 (N)] unit. The state-wide softwood inventory increase was driven by an increase in pine plantation volumes.

Generally, higher per acre concentrations of softwoods occurred in the south and southwestern counties, and lower concentrations occurred in Alabama's northern tier. Choctow County had the highest density of softwoods in the State, over 1,008 cubic feet per acre, while Limestone County had the lowest volume of softwoods per acre at 85 cubic feet. This trend is clearly shown in figure 11.

Loblolly pine remained the single most abundant softwood species. At almost 9 billion cubic feet, it accounted for 67 percent of the 2000 live softwood inventory (fig. 12).

Shortleaf, longleaf, and slash pines accounted for 9 percent, 8 percent, and 7 percent of the softwood total, respectively. Loblolly pine volume increased 39 percent for the period. Loblolly was the only southern yellow pine to experience an increase in volume. Cypress was the only other major species that increased in volume; it was up 44 percent.

The largest volume reductions were recorded for shortleaf (down 23 percent), followed by longleaf and slash pines (5 percent and 2 percent, respectively). Further declines for these three species were inevitable, as natural stands are harvested and artificially regenerated with more productive loblolly pine. All other pine species lost volume during the survey period.

Softwood all-live volume increases between 1990 and 2000 were recorded for all 2-inch diameter classes (fig. 13). Volume in the 6- to 10-inch diameter classes increased 26 percent. The volume increase in all other diameter classes (≥ 12 inches) was 10.5 percent. Trends illustrated in figure 13 show the softwood inventory continuing to register a buildup of larger trees (20+ inches), coupled with a shift in the curve by diameter class, moving from the 10- to 12-inch classes to the 8-inch class. Except in 1982, when the 12-inch diameter class was predominant, there has been more softwood volume in each diameter class for every survey since 1972. Primary forces driving these size class changes are the broad-scale establishment of planted pine stands and management techniques that favor shorter rotation cycles.

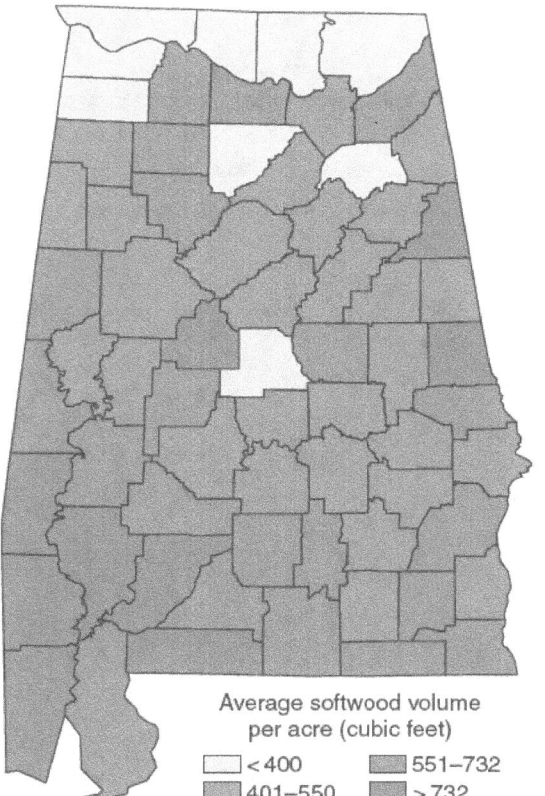

Figure 11—Average live softwood volume per acre of timberland by county, Alabama, 2000.

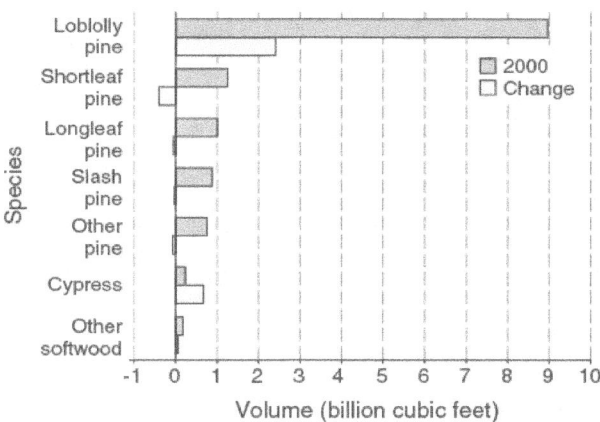

Figure 12—Volume of live softwoods on timberland by species and change in volume since 1990, Alabama.

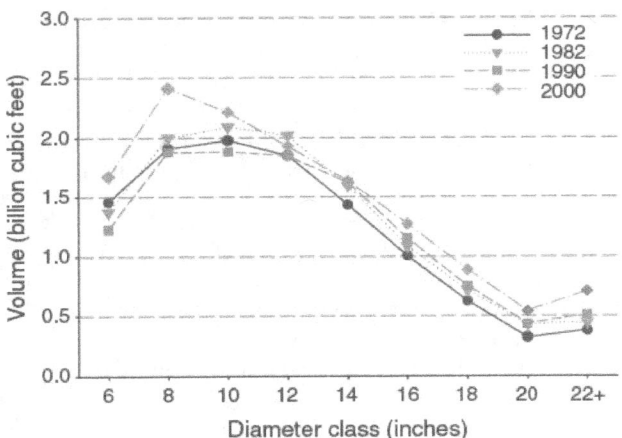

Figure 13—Volume of live softwoods on timberland by diameter class and survey year, Alabama.

The reasons behind the continuing accretion of volume in the larger size classes are uncertain. Nonetheless, this trend is not unique to Alabama; it is occurring everywhere in the South. Possible causes include the reduced availability of older stands, a gradual buildup of softwood volume in aging hardwood stands, and silvicultural practices, such as thinning, that enhance development of sawtimber products.

Hardwood Inventory

The hardwood growing stock inventory has continued to increase (fig. 7). Between 1990 and 2000 it increased 27 percent, from 12 billion cubic feet to 15 billion cubic feet. Hardwood totals for those two surveys represent the only inventories since 1953 to have shown more hardwood volume than softwood volume. Hardwood growing-stock volume has increased 149 percent over the last 50 years.

Eighty-three percent of live hardwood volume was on NIPF lands, 9 percent on lands managed by forest industry, and 8 percent on lands owned by public agencies (fig. 14). Since

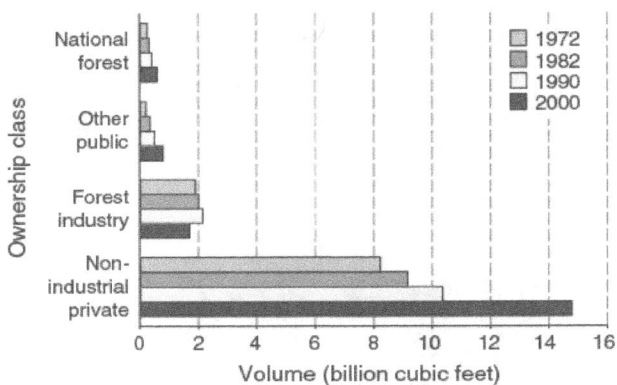

Figure 14—Volume of live hardwood on timberland by ownership class and survey year, Alabama.

Hardwood forests, such as this one in the Westervelt Management Area in Pickens County, account for 46 percent of the timberland area in Alabama. (photo by Kelvin J. Daniels)

1990, volume of live hardwoods had risen 43 percent on NIPF land and 49 percent on public land. In contrast, hardwood inventories had fallen by 22 percent on timberland controlled by forest industry, marking the first time since 1972 that hardwood volume decreased on any ownership.

Hardwood all-live volume has steadily increased in the oak-pine, oak-hickory, oak-gum-cypress, and natural longleaf-slash pine forest types over the previous four inventories (fig. 15). Hardwood volume more than doubled in the oak-hickory forest type and nearly doubled in the oak-gum-cypress type. Live hardwood volume increased in all types, except planted longleaf-slash pine stands, in which a slight decrease is shown.

Regionally, hardwood all-live tree volume increased in all six survey units (fig. 16); but the increase was most pronounced in the North unit, where volume was up 56 percent. The smallest increase in hardwood volume (19 percent) occurred in the West Central unit. Southeast Alabama contained the highest proportion (25 percent) of hardwood volume, while the Southwest South had the smallest proportion (8 percent).

Hardwood volume per acre estimates were higher in the northern counties and lower in the southern counties, just the

A stream in Colbert County. (photo by Kelvin J. Daniels)

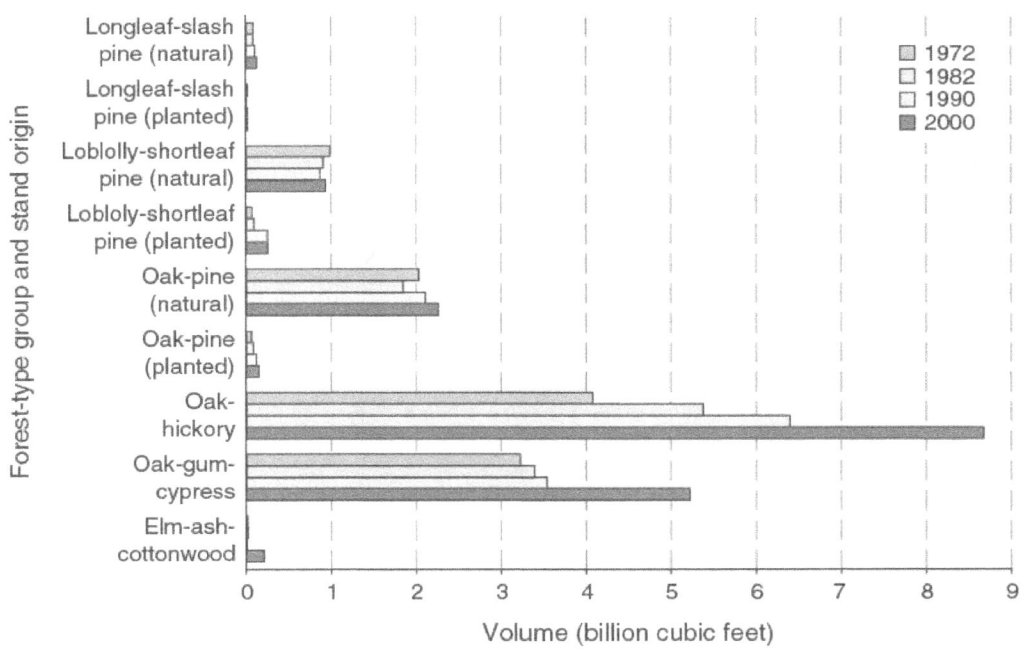

Figure 15—Volume of live hardwoods on timberland by forest-type group, stand origin, and survey year, Alabama.

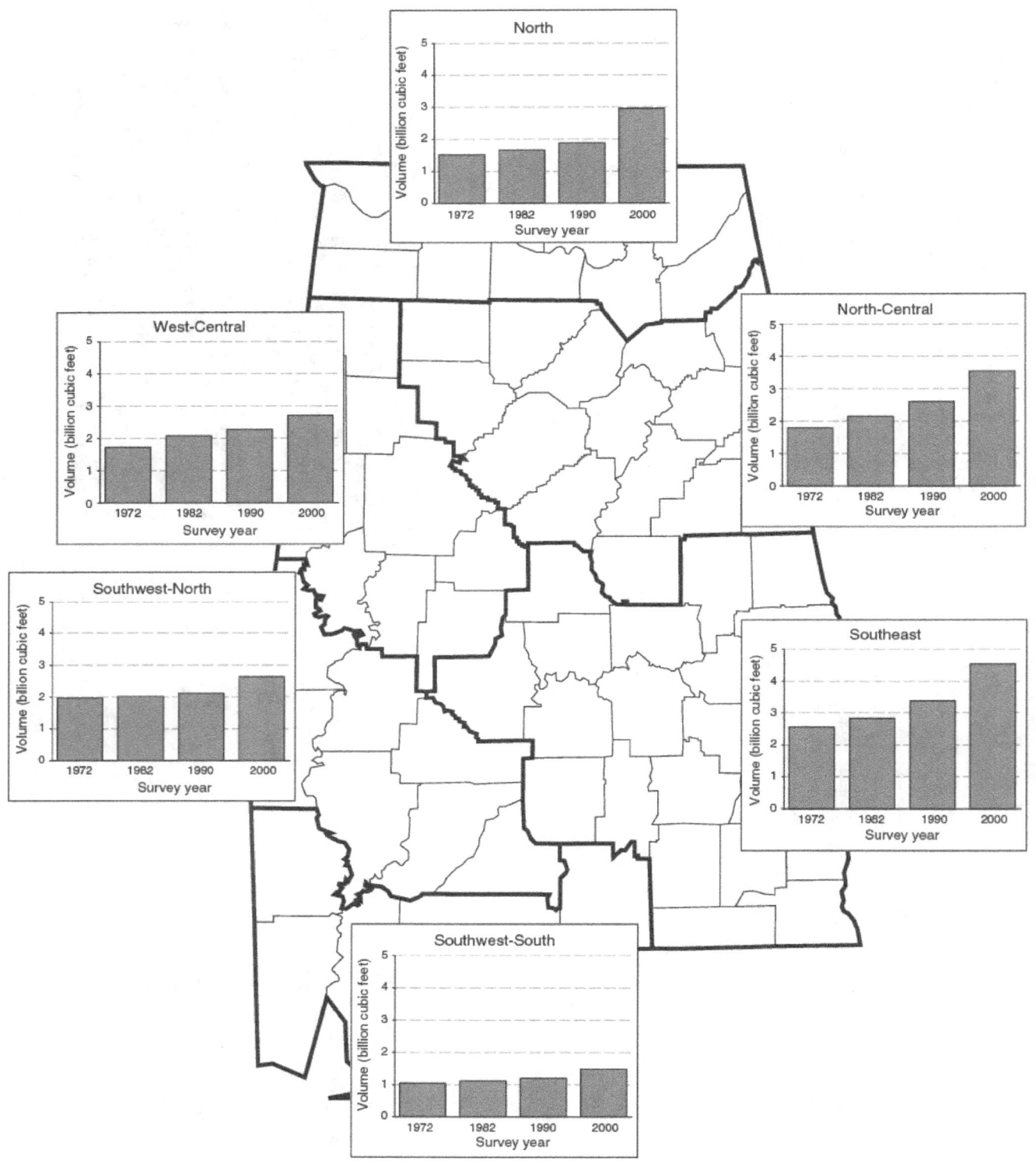

Figure 16—Volume of live hardwoods on timberland by survey unit for four inventory cycles, Alabama.

opposite of softwood estimates (fig. 17). Limestone County had over 2,062 cubic feet per acre, the highest per acre volume of all counties. Limestone County had the lowest softwood densities (fig. 11). The southernmost counties had the lowest concentration of hardwoods. Covington, Coffee, Mobile, and Escambia all had < 500 cubic feet per acre of hardwood volume.

The predominate hardwood species group in Alabama is other red oaks, which includes scarlet, southern red, shingle, laurel, water, pin, willow, and black oaks. These species constituted 4.0 billion cubic feet of all-live volume (fig. 18), representing a 36-percent increase since 1990. All major hardwood species groups registered increases in volume between 1990 and 2000. The most abundant single species was sweetgum, which constituted 2.6 billion cubic feet in all-live volume.

Hardwood volume increased across all diameter classes (fig. 19). The general shape of the curve shown in fig. 19 is the same as was shown in all other surveys except 1982. In that survey the "tail" of the curve was higher than it was in other surveys, i.e., there was more volume in the 6- to 8-inch diameter classes than in the other surveys. The pronounced peak in the 2000 survey's 8- to 12-inch classes is partially due to the maturation of the prior surveys' smaller diameter trees. Perhaps the most striking component of this figure is the almost 200 percent increase in hardwood volume for the larger diameter trees. The reasons for this are numerous, but many yet need to be identified and further studied.

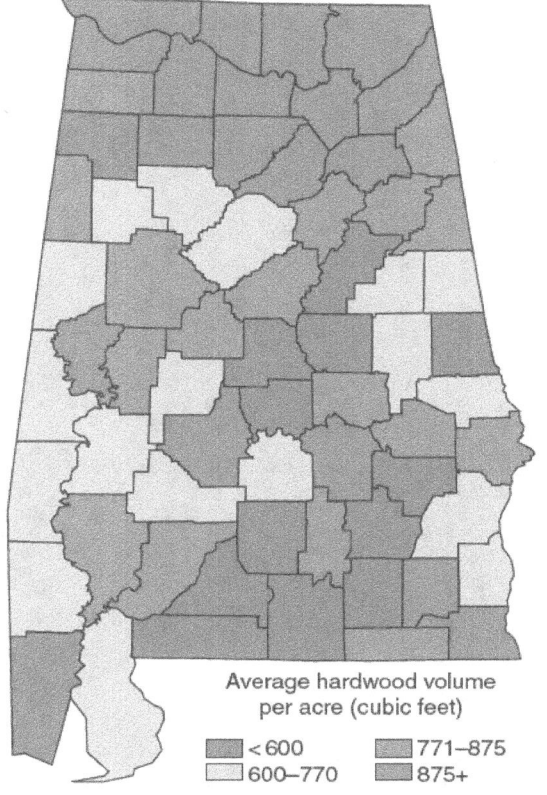

Average hardwood volume per acre (cubic feet)

■ < 600   ■ 771–875
□ 600–770   ■ 875+

Figure 17—Average live hardwood volume per acre of timberland by county, Alabama, 2000.

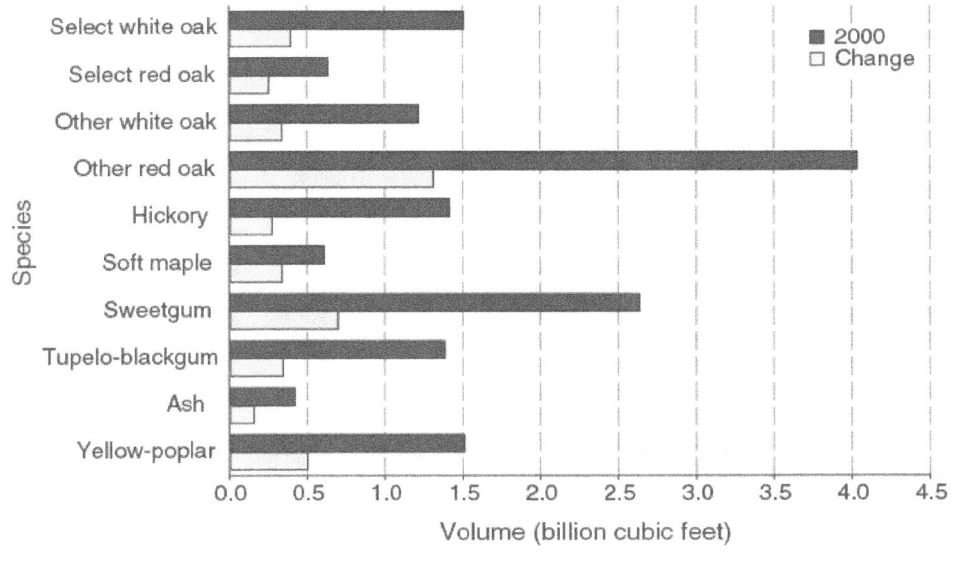

Figure 18—Volume of live hardwoods on timberland by species and change since 1990, Alabama.

15

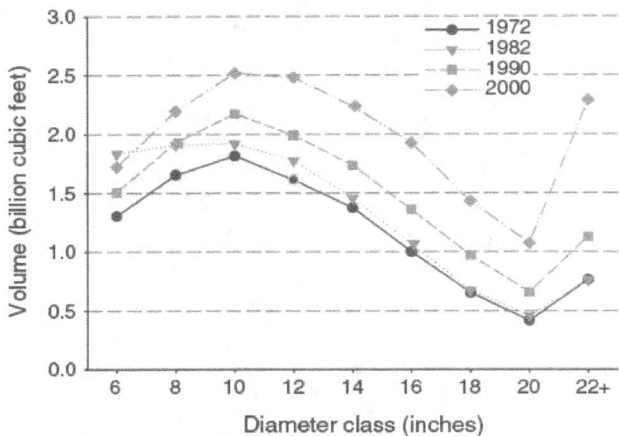

Figure 19—Volume of growing-stock hardwoods by diameter class and survey year, Alabama.

Crimson pitcher plant (photo by James Henderson, Gulf South Research Corporation, Bugwood.org)

Components of Inventory Change

Softwood Growth and Removals

Net annual growth of softwood growing stock averaged over 884 million cubic feet in the last remeasurement period (1990 to 2000), and had increased 34 percent between 1982 and 1989. The increase in softwood growth represents a continuing trend that began after the 1972 to 1981 survey period. Growing stock is the historical standard by which growth and removals are recorded. Long-term analysis requires use of the growing stock designation, though current protocols emphasize all-live trees. For example, during the 1953 to 1961 period, only growing-stock estimates were recorded. Alabama's softwood growing-stock growth in 2000 was at its highest recorded level (fig. 20). In contrast to trends in softwood growth, removals of softwood growing stock escalated steadily over the previous five survey periods. By 2000, the average annual removals of growing-stock softwoods had increased almost 24 percent over the previous inventory. The current growth-to-removals ratio for growing-stock softwoods is almost 1-to-1, compared to 0.91-to-1 in the previous period. Except during the 1982 to 1989 period, softwood growth has always equaled or exceeded removals.

Alabama reached a peak in growing-stock growth during the 1963 to 1971 remeasurement period, largely because areas of abandoned farmland had reverted to forest naturally or had been planted during the 1950s and 1960s (fig. 20). Between 1972 and 1981, large areas of mature pine stands were being harvested, resulting in a 17 percent decrease in net growth. As older stands with high volumes were

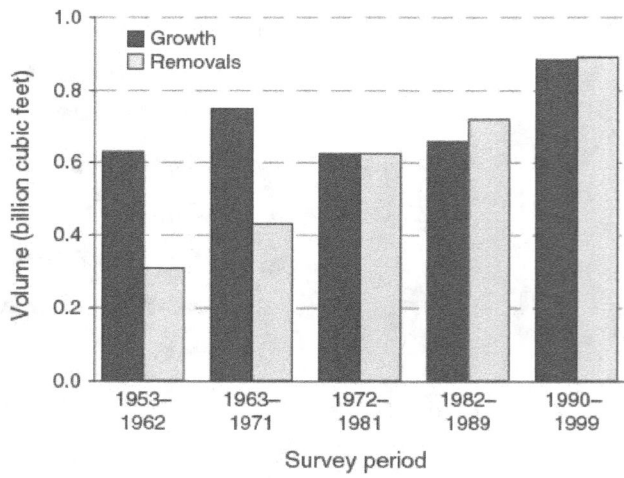

Figure 20—Average annual growth and annual removals of softwood growing stock on timberland by survey period, Alabama.

16

replaced by younger stands, overall growth declined. (Trees do not contribute to growth until they reach the SRS-FIA merchantability standard of 5.0 inches diameter at breast height [d.b.h.]). Between 1982 and 1989, softwood growth was up by 5 percent. While harvesting increased, ingrowth from stands established in the 1970s and 1980s boosted softwood volume (McWilliams 1992).

Alabama's softwood growth is at an all-time high, primarily due to intense forest management practices and continuing conversion of abandoned farmlands to forest. Alabama's Conservation Reserve Program (CRP) established about 100,000 acres of new timberland per year between 1991 and 1999. Stands whose size-class entered the 5.0-inch threshold greatly contributed to softwood ingrowth.

The various components of softwood growth are summarized in table 3. By 2000, softwood survivor growth, which is the increment of all-live trees ≥5.0 inches d.b.h., made up 51 percent of Alabama's total gross growth. Ingrowth,

Table 3—Components of average annual change of live trees by survey unit and species group, Alabama 1990 to 2000

Survey unit and species group	Survivor growth	Ingrowth	Growth on ingrowth	Growth on cut	Growth on mortality	Timber removals	Mortality	Gross growth	Net growth	Net change
	- million cubic feet -									*percent*
Southwest-South										
Softwood	62.45	18.02	18.99	22.73	4.70	100.43	17.49	126.79	109.30	8.87
Hardwood	45.93	10.63	8.26	5.42	2.53	39.74	16.46	72.76	56.30	16.56
Total	108.38	28.64	27.25	28.15	7.23	140.17	33.95	199.55	165.60	25.43
Southwest-North										
Softwood	107.90	25.06	32.66	54.32	7.01	190.05	23.14	226.84	203.70	13.65
Hardwood	88.47	16.13	16.62	12.77	4.25	77.10	24.45	138.25	113.80	36.70
Total	196.37	41.19	49.28	67.10	11.26	267.15	47.59	365.09	317.50	50.35
Southeast										
Softwood	108.95	48.30	72.93	87.32	14.56	279.95	51.56	331.96	280.40	0.45
Hardwood	145.14	27.16	18.40	23.31	8.10	128.44	45.21	222.11	176.90	48.46
Total	254.09	75.45	91.32	110.63	22.66	408.40	96.77	554.07	457.30	48.90
West-Central										
Softwood	59.77	25.57	37.28	45.40	7.77	156.05	24.80	175.80	151.00	-5.05
Hardwood	85.60	14.72	10.63	15.61	5.33	92.04	30.99	131.89	100.90	8.86
Total	145.36	40.29	47.92	61.02	13.09	248.10	55.78	307.68	251.90	3.81
North-Central										
Softwood	75.14	27.48	31.19	34.21	9.50	139.72	35.62	177.42	141.80	2.08
Hardwood	112.73	22.83	13.41	15.43	5.16	89.32	30.66	169.56	138.90	49.58
Total	187.87	50.31	44.60	49.64	14.66	229.04	66.28	346.98	280.70	51.66
North										
Softwood	21.75	6.12	4.12	14.45	4.53	47.77	14.28	50.88	36.60	-11.17
Hardwood	88.15	14.92	10.23	6.83	3.33	38.11	20.07	123.47	103.40	65.30
Total	109.91	21.04	14.35	21.28	7.87	85.87	34.34	174.34	140.00	54.13
All units										
Softwood	435.96	150.54	197.17	258.44	48.07	913.97	166.88	1,089.68	922.80	8.83
Hardwood	566.02	106.38	77.55	79.38	28.70	464.75	167.83	858.03	690.20	225.45
Total	1,001.98	256.92	274.72	337.82	76.77	1,378.73	334.71	1,947.71	1,613.00	234.27

Numbers in columns may not sum to totals due to rounding.

the net volume of live trees reaching 5.0 inches d.b.h. during the survey period, accounted for 13 percent of gross growth, which is the sum of all components (survivor, ingrowth, growth on ingrowth, growth on cut, and growth on mortality).

Net change is net growth minus timber removals. A positive net change indicates that average annual growth exceeds removals, while a negative net change indicates that removals exceed growth. Alabama's statewide softwood and hardwood net change totals are positive. This is a dramatic turnaround from the 1982 to 1989 inventory, which reported a negative net change for softwoods. The only incidences of negative net change for softwoods occur in the West Central and North survey units.

All-live softwood growth increased across all ownership categories: on NIPF land it was up 45 percent to 612 million cubic feet; national forests recorded a 76 percent increase, to 24 million cubic feet; and all other public lands increased growth by 118 percent to 17 million cubic feet (fig. 21). Forest industry softwood growth was up 29 percent to 269 million cubic feet, about the same as during the 1972 to 1981 period. These growth increases reversed declines measured in earlier survey periods.

While softwood growth trends have fluctuated between and among ownerships and survey periods, all-live softwood removals have steadily increased (fig. 22). After 1990 all-live softwood removals increased for industry and NIPF lands, by 32 and 22 percent, respectively. At the same time, removals from national forest lands had risen 44 percent, while softwood removals on other public lands increased by 16 percent. Comparing all-live softwood growth to removals by ownership reveals that lands controlled by private entities (forest industry and NIPF) currently have growth-to-removal ratios of almost 1-to-1, while all public controlled lands presently have growth-to-removals ratios slightly > 1.3-to-1.0.

Over the past 40 years, similar trends in all-live softwood growth and removals were observed in each of the six survey regions. From 1963 to 1971, net annual growth exceeded removals by large margins in all survey units (fig. 23). From 1972 to 1981, the gap between growth and removals narrowed and even reversed in the Southwest South, Southwest North, and Southeast units. The 1982 to 1989 period continued the trend set in the previous inventory, in which growth-to-removals ratios either approached unity (1-to-1) or removals exceeded growth.

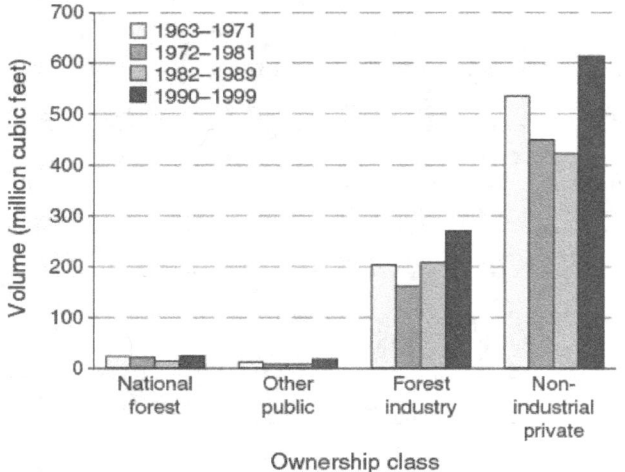

Figure 21—Growth of live softwoods on timberland by ownership class and survey period, Alabama.

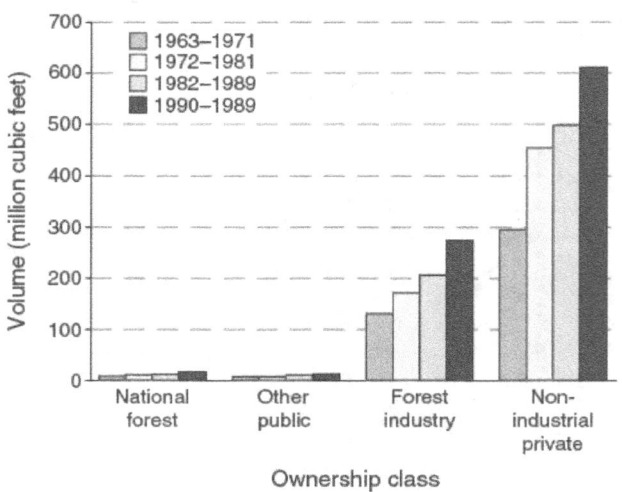

Figure 22—Average annual removals of live softwoods on timberland by ownership class and survey period, Alabama.

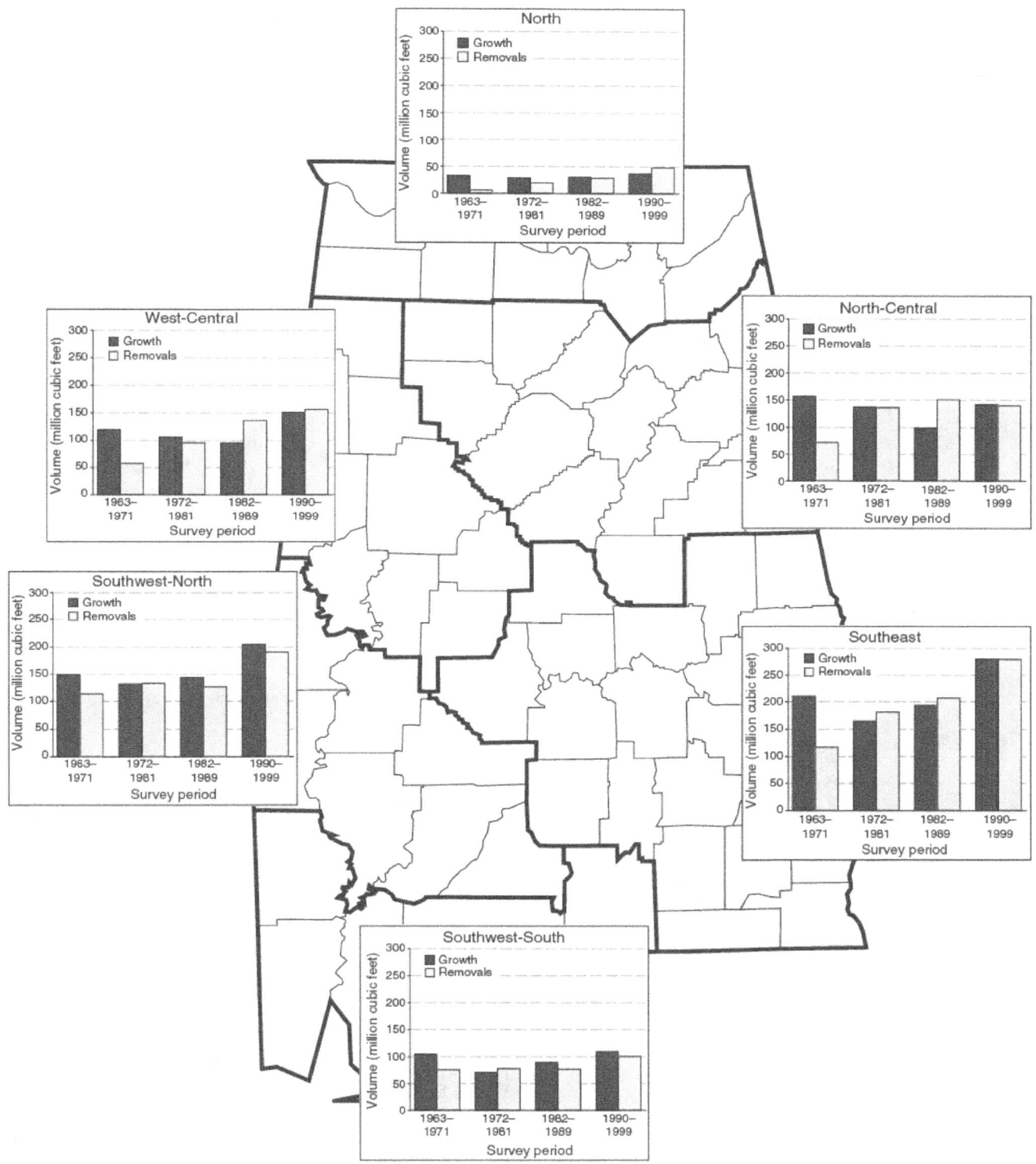

Figure 23—Average annual growth and removals of live softwoods on timberland by survey unit and survey period, Alabama.

Figure 24 shows an increase in softwood removals across all diameter classes, the largest occurring in the 6- through 12-inch diameter classes. Removals in the 6-inch diameter class increased 86 percent between the two most recent survey periods, but the 8-, 10-, and 12-inch classes went up 47, 30, and 16 percent, respectively. This increase in removals, for these specific diameter classes, may help explain why the volume of the 12-inch class softwoods was less than in the previous inventory (fig. 13). However, softwood volume and growth have increased the past 30+ years due to increases in timberland area, as well as improved stocking, management, and forest vigor.

Hardwood Growth and Removals

Average annual growth of hardwood growing stock increased more than 5 percent to 596 million cubic feet per year after 1989. The average net annual growth of hardwoods represents a half-century upward trend (fig. 25). Likewise, removals of hardwood growing stock have steadily increased since the 1963 to 1971 inventory. The growth-to-removals ratios for Alabama hardwoods always have exceeded 1.46-to-1. The latest survey reveals hardwood growth increasing 5 percent, and removals rising almost 10 percent.

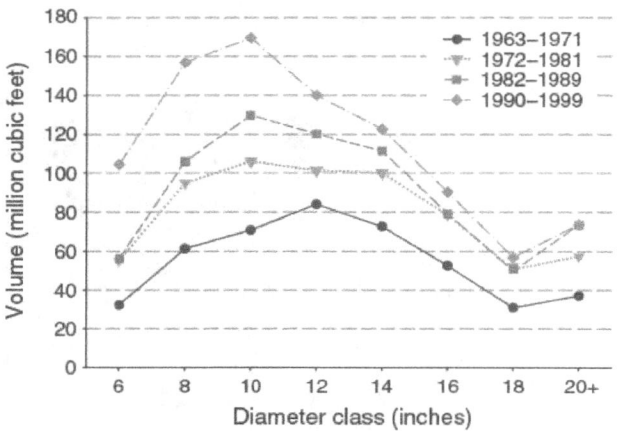

Figure 24—Average annual removals of live softwoods on timberland by diameter class and survey period, Alabama.

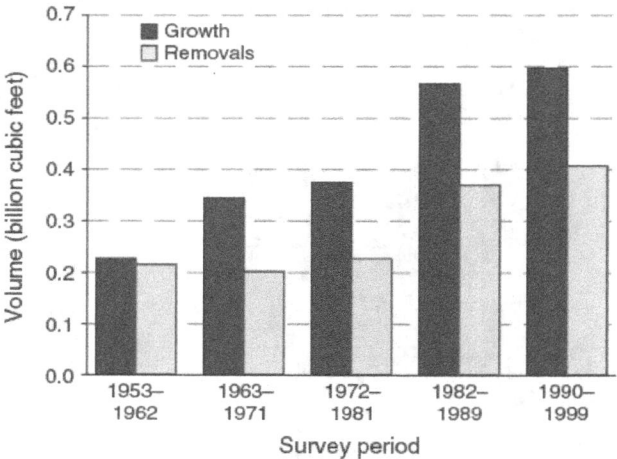

Figure 25—Average annual growth and annual removals of hardwood growing stock on timberland by survey period, Alabama.

An oak-hickory stand in Randolph County. (photo by David Stephens, Bugwood.org)

20

All live hardwood growth has increased steadily across all ownerships except forest industry (fig. 26). Average annual live hardwood growth on NIPF lands rose 32 percent to 577 million cubic feet per year. Hardwood growth on national forest and other public lands increased 46 and 33 percent, respectively.

Annual removals of live hardwoods on NIPF lands rose 28 percent to 371 million cubic feet per year (fig. 27). The only other ownership to have an increase in hardwood removals is other public, which went up 28 percent. Hardwood removals on national forest and forest industry owned lands decreased almost 10 percent each. Average annual growth-to-removal ratios for live hardwoods by ownership show that hardwood growth always has exceeded removals for all ownerships except forest industry. By 2000, the highest hardwood growth-to-removal ratio occurred on national forest lands (5.3-to-1.0), followed by other public (3.9-to-1.0), and NIPF (1.6-to-1.0).

Hardwood net growth increased in every survey unit (fig. 28). Removals increased in all survey units except the Southwest-North unit, which experienced a 9.75 percent decline. Historical hardwood growth-to-removal ratios for all survey units show that growth always has exceeded removals. The margin of growth over removals was highest for the North survey unit (2.71-to-1.0) and lowest in the West Central survey unit (1.09-to-1.0). Hardwood growth-to-removals ratios ranged from 1.4-to-1.0 and 1.5-to-1.0 for the other units.

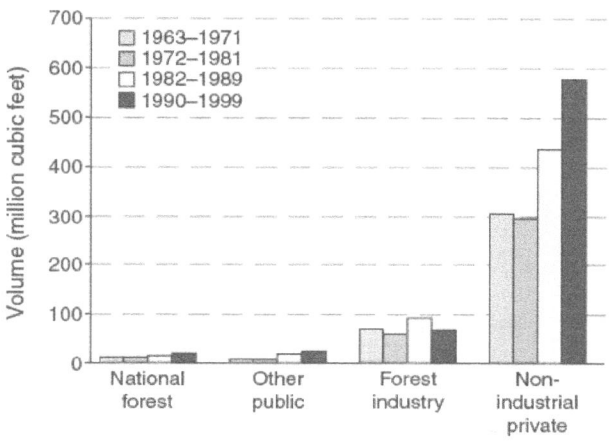

Figure 26—Average annual growth of live hardwoods on timberland by ownership class and survey period, Alabama.

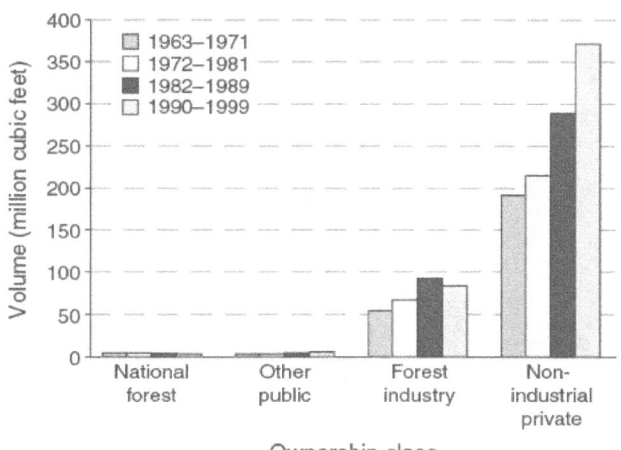

Figure 27—Average annual removals of live hardwoods on timberland by ownership class and survey period, Alabama.

Bobcats such as this one, play an important role in Alabama's forested ecosystems. (photo by Terry Spivey, Bugwood.org)

21

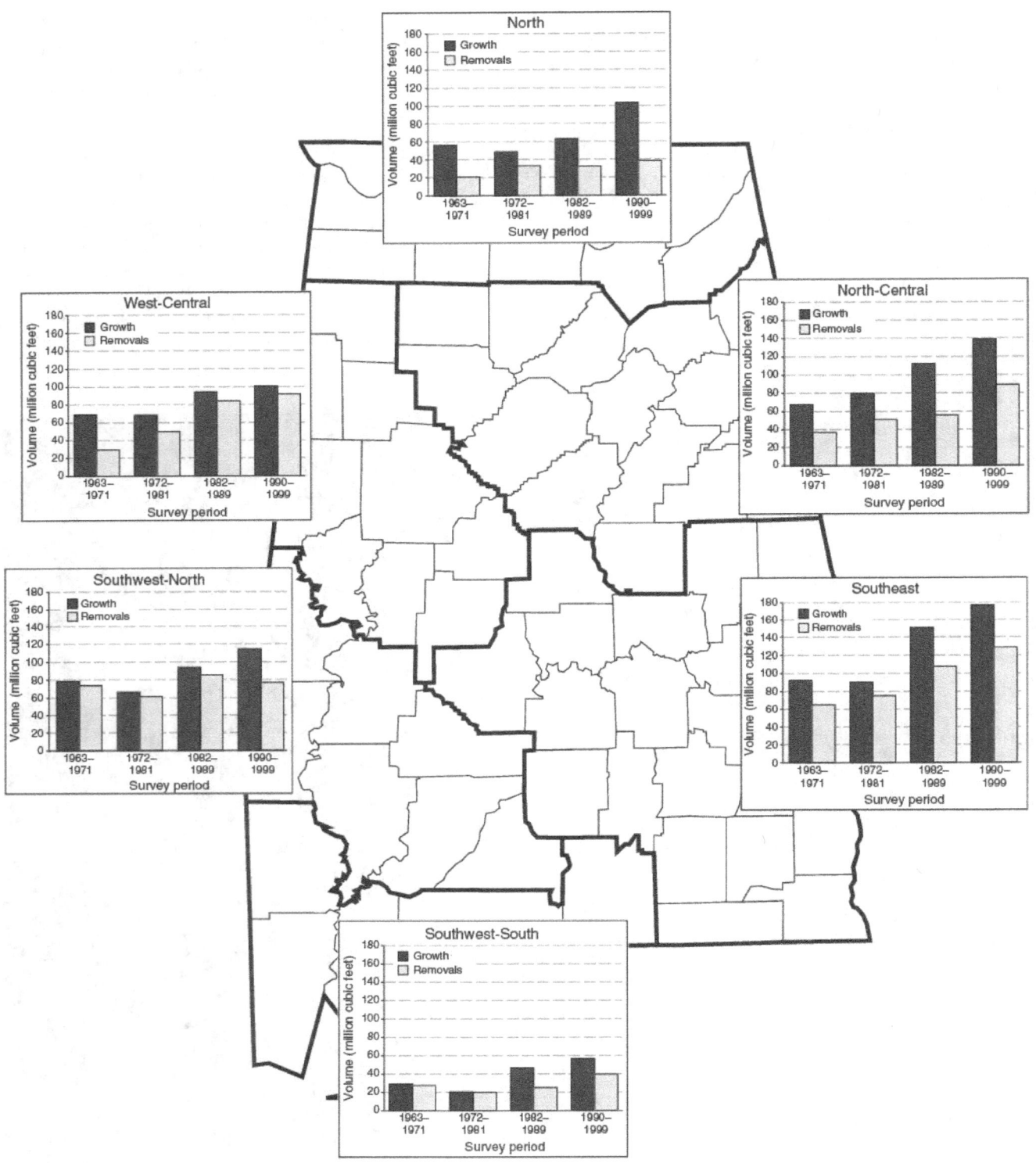

Figure 28—Average annual growth and removals of live hardwoods on timberland by survey unit for four remeasurement periods, Alabama.

The increase in average annual hardwood removals has occurred across all diameter classes, but especially the 8- and 10-inch classes (fig. 29), continuing a trend that began sometime during the 1982 to 1989 survey period. Then, hardwood removals were attributed to increased demand, mainly in the manufacture of pulp and paper (McWilliams 1992). With recent changes to Alabama's infrastructure, construction of the Tennessee-Tombigbee Waterway, and changes in the pulping process, which allow for higher percentages of hardwood to be used, demand has increased. Hardwoods in the 6- to 12-inch diameter classes are affected most and, therefore, constitute a greater proportion of hardwood removals.

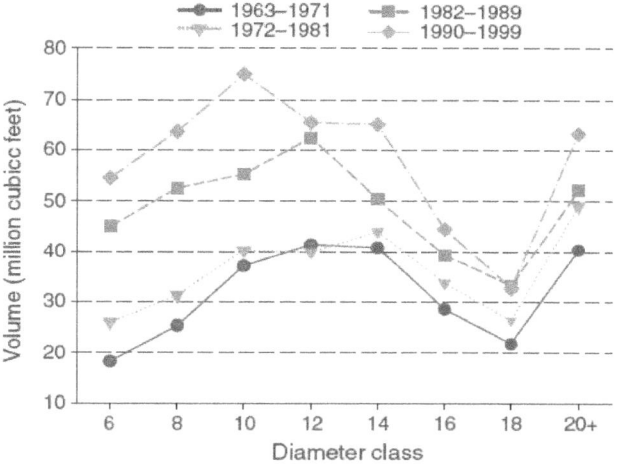

Figure 29—Average annual removals of live hardwoods on timberland, Alabama.

Timber Product Output

Alabama's forest products industry is an important component of the State's economy. Forestry, logging, and wood products manufacturing contribute more than $12 billion annually to the State's economy in terms of value of shipments. Alabama's forestry manufacturing amounted to about 18 percent of the State's total manufacturing (Alabama Forestry Commission 2002). In 2000, more than 180 sawmills, pulpwood mills, and other primary wood-processing plants were distributed across the State, and nearly 1,700 secondary manufacturers directly employed nearly 64,500 individuals. These businesses had a combined payroll of more than $2 billion.

According to IMPLAN (IMpact Analysis for PLANning), a model generated by the Forest Service, U.S. Department of Agriculture (Abt and others 2002), the total economic value of Alabama's forests in 2001 was about $18.6 billion, a figure that includes all activities associated with the forest products industry, e.g., direct, indirect, and induced effects resulting from industry operations. Nontimber benefits, such as specialty forest products, recreation, water, wildlife habitat, and esthetic values, also contribute greatly to the State's economy and well-being of the general population.

Timber Product Output and Removals

This section presents estimates of annual product output and timber removals for the period 1990 through 1999. However, estimates of timber product output (TPO) and plant residues were obtained from a 1999 canvass of all

Hardwood forests, such as this one in Marshall County, are not always dominated by a single size class, but have a diverse range of tree sizes and species. (photo by Kelvin J. Daniels)

primary wood-using mills in the State (Howell and others 2002). Forest industry surveys typically are conducted every 2 years by personnel from the Alabama Forestry Commission and the Southern Research Station. These data are used to augment FIA's annual inventory of timber removals by providing proportions of removals that are used for various products. Individual studies are necessary to track trends and changes in product output levels. Total product output is the sum of the volume of roundwood products from all sources (growing stock and other sources) and the volume of plant byproducts, or the mill residues.

Total output of timber products, including domestic fuelwood, amounted to >1.7 billion cubic feet in 1999. Seventy-three percent of the total output was from round-wood products; the remainder was from plant byproducts. At 1.3 billion cubic feet, softwood species provided 74 percent of the total product output volume. Hardwoods provided the remaining 26 percent, or 0.4 billion cubic feet of total output.

Pulpwood has been and remains the primary industrial wood product produced by Alabama's mills. Total pulpwood production was 782 million cubic feet and accounted for 46 percent of the State's total TPO volume. Saw-log volume, used mainly for dimension lumber, totaled 429 million cubic feet and accounted for one-quarter of the total output volume. Total fuelwood, which includes domestic fuelwood and mill residue such as bark and sawdust used for industrial fuelwood, ranked third at 17 percent, or 296 million cubic feet. Eighty-nine percent, or more than 264 million cubic feet, were used for industrial purposes. Veneer, which includes pine plywood, totaled 109 million cubic feet and constituted another 6 percent of total TPO volume. Miscellaneous products such as poles, posts, and composite panels were nearly 94 million cubic feet, the remaining 6 percent of total output.

Output of roundwood products (including fuelwood) totaled 1.24 billion cubic feet for 1999. Ninety-two percent, or 1.14 billion cubic feet, of the roundwood products volume came from growing-stock trees, split between sawtimber (72 percent) and poletimber (28 percent). Other sources, which include cull trees, salvable dead, as well as stumps and tops of harvested trees, were 97 million cubic feet, or 8 percent of the total roundwood TPO.

Total timber removals between 1990 and 1999 include the volume of roundwood products, logging residues (unused portions of trees, which are left in the woods), and other removals (removals attributed to land clearing or land

A daffodil along a roadside. (photo by Andrew J. Hartsell)

use changes) from growing stock and nongrowing stock sources. Removals from all sources, for both softwoods and hardwoods combined, totaled 1.4 billion cubic feet. Softwoods accounted for 67 percent of total removals. Volume used for roundwood products totaled 1.24 billion cubic feet, or 86 percent, of total removals. Logging residues and other removals amounted to 131 million cubic feet (9 percent) and 73 million cubic feet (5 percent), respectively.

Specialty Forest Products

Specialty forest products or nontimber forest products (NTFP) have been harvested from Alabama's forests for many years. Although these products contribute a much smaller percentage to the overall economy than traditional forest products, they provide millions of dollars to many local rural economies. Many of these products are collected with very little forest disturbance and range from edible products (fruits, nuts, mushrooms, and ramps), to medicinal-type products (ginseng and bloodroot), ornamental products (galax, pine tips for garlands, and grapevines), landscape products (pine straw and native plants), and specialty woods (burl and crotch wood for fine crafts).

According to a survey of county extension agents, as of April 2003, Alabama had a total of 1,411 NTFP enterprises (Chamberlain and Predny 2003). The floral and decorative products, specialty woods, and landscape products categories each accounted for 27 percent of the NTFP enterprises with 377 firms in each of these categories. The edible products category had 221, or 16 percent, of the NTFP enterprises, while medicinal products comprised 58, or 4 percent, of the firms. Alabama accounted for 6 percent of NTFP enterprises in the southern region.

Stand Structure

Three units of measure are used to describe forest structure: number of trees per acre, basal area per acre, and stocking. Number of trees per acre and basal area per acre both indicate stand density. Stocking is a measure expressed as number or volume onsite—relative to a standard that represents "full" occupancy.

Number of Trees

Comparing the average number of trees per acre by diameter class (or stand table) portrays changes in average stand conditions. Shifts in the 2000 hardwood stand table (fig. 30) are fairly dramatic. Almost all diameter classes increased in trees per acre. The only diameter class that showed a decrease from the last survey is the 4-inch class. The current estimate is only 2.5 percent less than in 1990. All other hardwood diameter classes experienced increases in the average number of trees per acre over the past 10 years, the smallest being a 4 percent increase in the 6-inch diameter class. Each successive diameter class experienced increases in the average number of hardwood trees per acre. This same hardwood pattern holds true when the current stand data is compared to 1972. There are small decreases in the average number of trees per acre in the 2- and 4-inch classes, and gradual increases for each successive 2-inch diameter class.

Changes in the softwood stand table are even more pronounced than those in the hardwood table. All softwood diameter classes showed an increase in the average number of trees per acre after 1990 (fig. 31). However, unlike

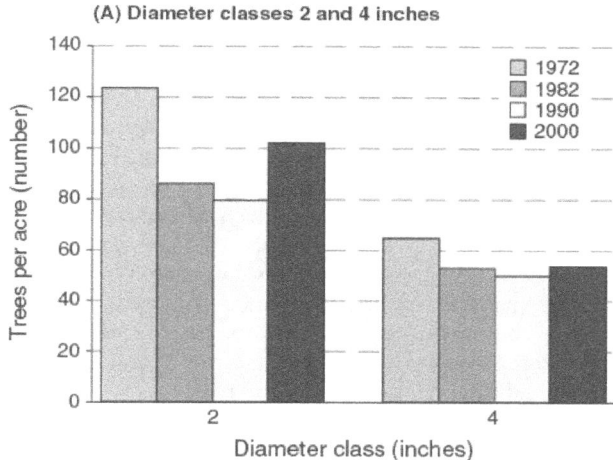

(A) Diameter classes 2 and 4 inches

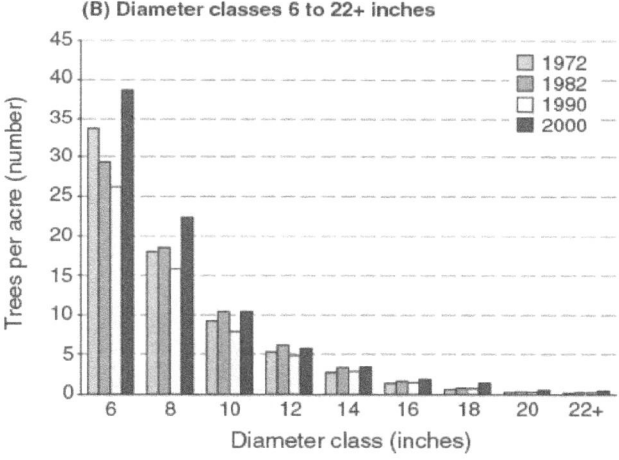

(B) Diameter classes 6 to 22+ inches

Figure 31—Average number of live softwoods per acre of timberland by diameter class and survey year (A) diameter classes 2 and 4 inches, and (B) diameter classes 6 to 22+ inches, Alabama.

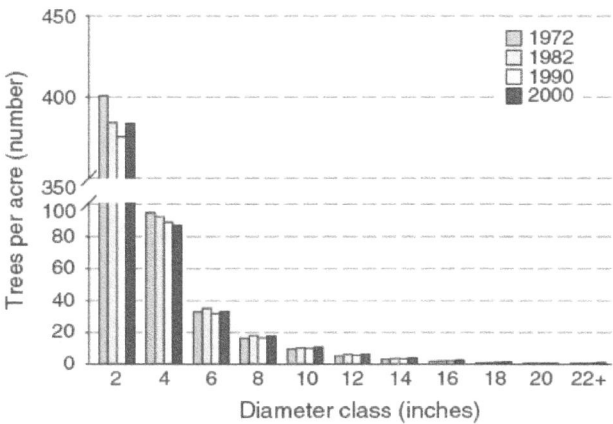

Figure 30—Average number of live hardwoods per acre of timberland by diameter class and survey year, Alabama.

hardwoods, increases in the average number of softwoods have no distinct pattern across diameter classes. The 6-, 8-, 10-, 18-, 20-, and 22-inch classes had 10-year increases >40 percent, while the 4-, 12-, and 14-inch classes showed increases <20 percent. The long-term trend reveals decreases in the smaller diameter classes (2- and 4-inch) and increases in the larger trees. Again, there is no distinct pattern, as certain diameter classes showed huge increases (125 percent increase in 18-inch softwoods), while other classes have a smaller growth rate (8 percent increase for the 12-inch class).

Basal Area

An average acre of timberland in Alabama contains 82.4 square feet of all-live basal area, of which 61 percent is hardwood and 39 percent is softwood (fig. 32). This represents an 11 percent increase during the survey period—from 74.3 square feet in 1990. Over the past 10 years, average softwood basal area has increased 13 percent, while hardwoods have risen 9.5 percent. Long-term analysis (1972 to 2000) reveals the changes in average basal area per acre for hardwoods to be +7 percent, while for softwoods it is -2 percent. Softwood basal area is highest in pine forest types, while average hardwood basal area is highest in the oak-gum-cypress forest type.

All-live basal area decreased slightly in the 2- and 4-inch diameter classes, and increased in all others (fig. 33). Such increases were greater for larger trees. Average basal area of the 6- to 12-inch classes rose between 4 and 6 percent, while trees ≥ 18 inches rose at least 76 percent over the past 10 years. The 1972 to 2000 trend reveals increases across the larger diameter classes as well, although the average basal area of 6-inch trees has not attained the level found in 1972.

Alabama's forests are the home for many wildlife species. (photo by Andrew J. Hartsell)

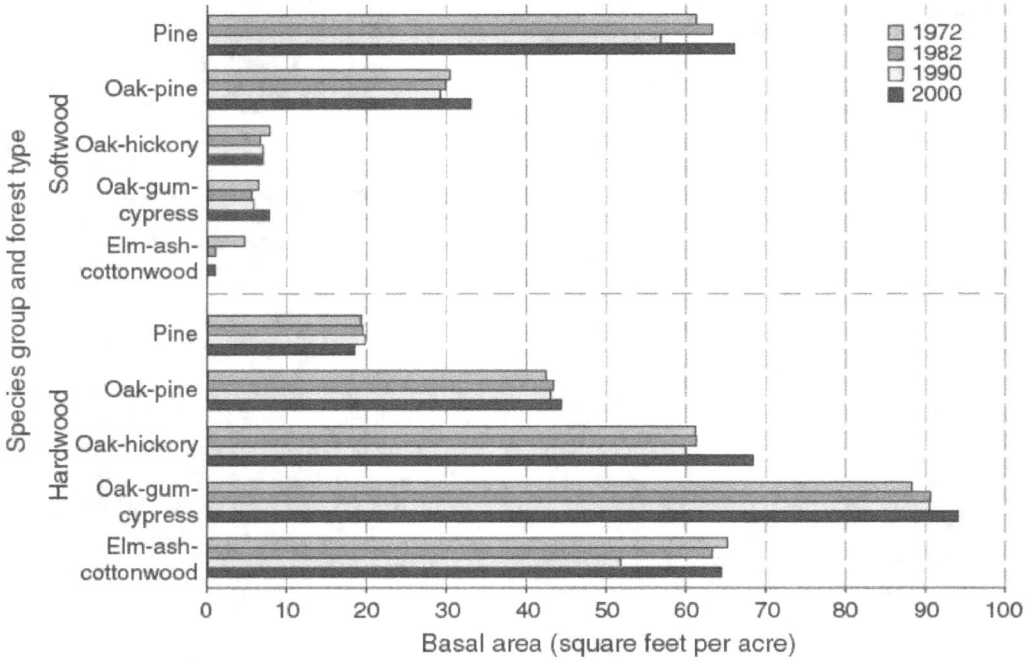

Figure 32—Basal area of live trees on timberland by species group, forest type, and survey year, Alabama.

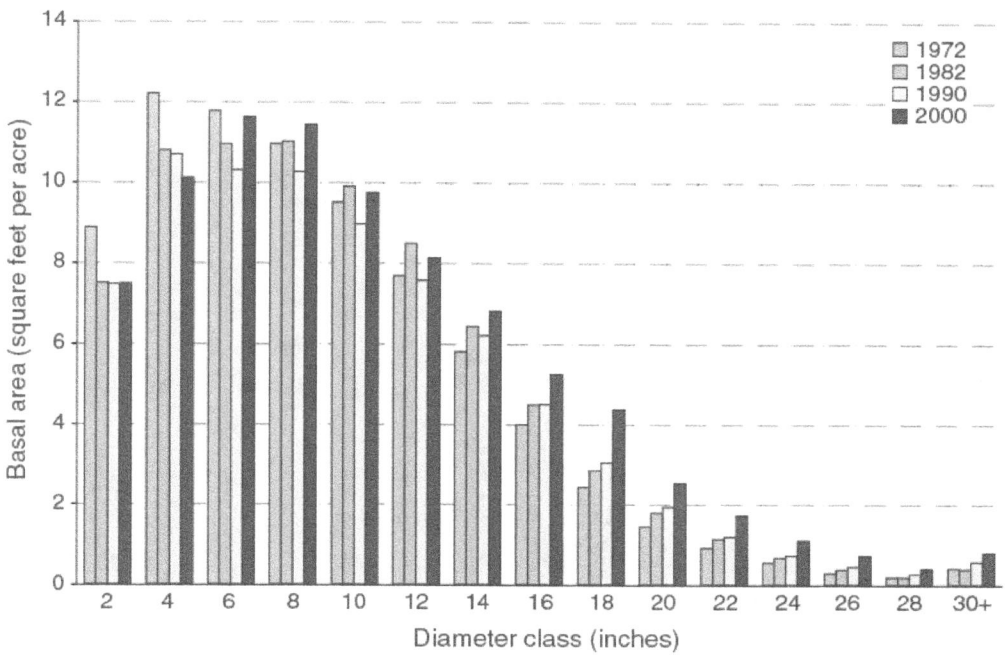

Figure 33—Average basal area per acre of live trees on timberland by survey year, Alabama.

Figure 34 illustrates geographic differences in all-live basal area distribution. While characteristics of basal area profiles for the entire State generally apply in each geographic region, a somewhat different structure is apparent for stands in the southern units. These profiles reflect a predominance of southern pine plantations, where most basal area is concentrated in smaller diameter trees and younger stands. The northern units have older hardwood stands and are subject to less intensive management.

Stocking

For analytical purposes, timberland is grouped into five classes according to the stocking of live trees: nonstocked (<16.7 percent stocked), poorly stocked (16.7 to 59 percent stocked), optimally stocked (60 to 99 percent stocked), fully stocked (100 to 130 percent stocked), and overstocked (>130 percent stocked). Trends in distribution of timberland in these five classes have changed considerably over

Healthy forests benefit not only the environment, but traditional timber and nontimber industries as well. (photo by Kelvin J. Daniels)

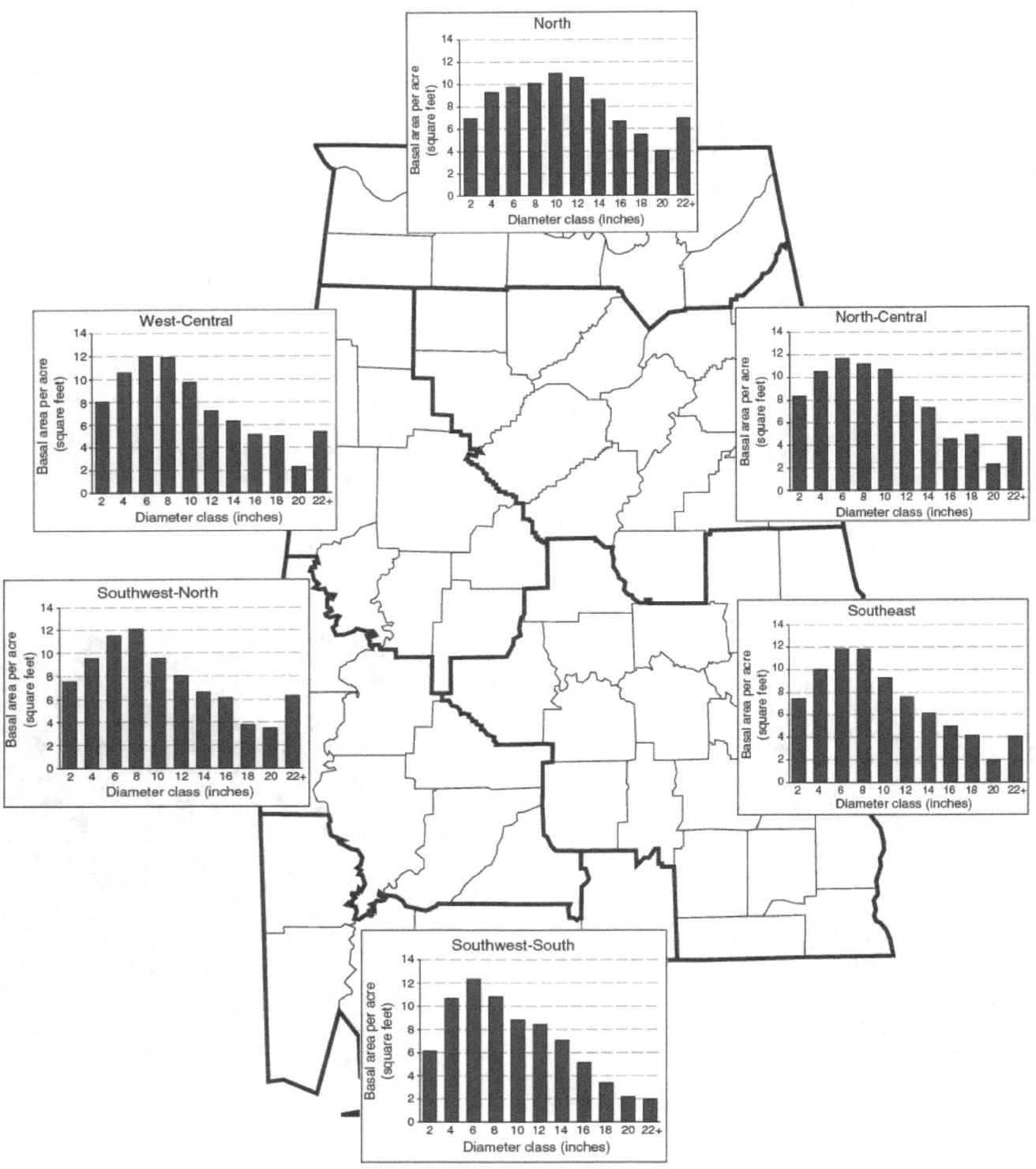

Figure 34—Average basal area of live trees on timberland by diameter class and survey unit in Alabama, 2000.

the past four inventory periods (fig. 35). While the area of nonstocked timberland has increased 81 percent, this class has always represented < 1.8 percent of the total timberland area. Figure 35 shows that the area of poorly and optimally stocked stands has decreased, while the area of fully and overstocked stands increased. In 1972, 53 percent of timberland was optimally stocked, while only 4 percent of the stands were overstocked. The latest inventory shows a reversal of this; only 18 percent of timberland area is in optimally stocked stands, and 41 percent is classified as overstocked. Overstocked stands account for more area than any other stocking class. The area of Alabama's overstocked stands has increased over 1,000 percent since 1972.

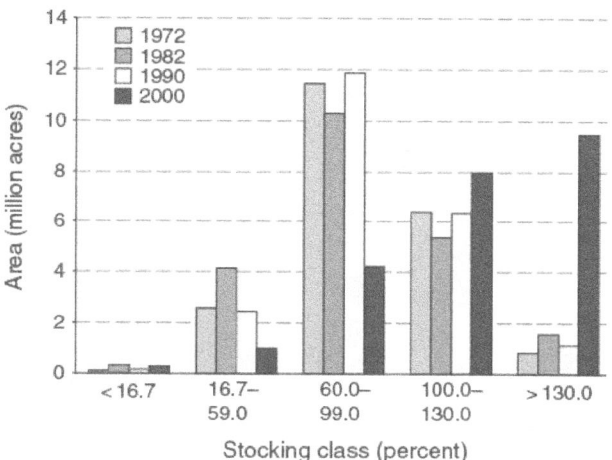

Figure 35—Area of timberland by stocking class and survey year, Alabama.

Effects of Pine Plantations on Alabama's Forests

Possible long-term effects of southern pine plantations are subject to interpretation. These forests increase the efficiency of timber production but also alter forest structure and composition, as well as wildlife habitat.

Most of the all-live volume in Alabama's plantations is in softwood species. Of the 4.7 billion cubic feet of wood in plantations, 92 percent is softwood; and 82 percent of that is in loblolly pine. Conversely, natural stands are composed

of only 36 percent softwoods. Most of Alabama's hardwood volume, 97 percent, is in natural stands (table 4).

Alabama's plantations are productive; the growth-to-volume ratio for plantation softwoods is 10 percent. (The growth of plantation softwoods, 459.6 million cubic feet per year, divided by the total softwood volume, 4,366.5 million cubic feet equals 10 percent.) The removals-to-volume ratio for plantation softwoods is 8.5 percent, while the mortality-to-volume ratio is 0.75 percent. Thus, softwood plantations grow 10 percent of their total all-live volume annually, while 8.5 percent is removed each year. In 2000, growth of plantation softwoods exceeded removals. Plantations harbor 52 percent of all softwood growth across the State, despite the fact that they account for only 34 percent of the total softwood volume, and plantations occur on only 24 percent of the timberland.

In natural stands, the growth-to-volume ratio for all species is 4.2 percent, while the removals-to-volume ratio is 3.6 percent. Softwoods in natural stands have a growth-to-volume ratio and removals-to-volume ratio of 5 and 6 percent, respectively. Currently, removals of all live softwoods exceed growth in natural stands.

Natural stands have more volume due to the large amount of area they occupy. However, the diameter distributions

Prescribed fire is often used to control understory vegetation in pine plantations. (photo by Ricky Layson, Ricky Layson Photography)

Table 4—Volume, average annual growth, average annual removals, and average annual mortality of all-live trees on timberland by species and stand origin, Alabama 2000

Species group	Stand origin							
	Natural				Planted			
	Volume	Growth	Removals	Mortality	Volume	Growth	Removals	Mortality
	thousand cubic feet							
Softwood								
Longleaf pine	924,996.9	33,420.6	37,818.0	7,597.7	72,627.3	5,273.8	16,829.1	697.2
Slash pine	571,245.3	25,410.9	36,148.6	6,920.5	296,860.3	29,433.4	23,600.3	3,375.0
Shortleaf pine	1,154,244.1	39,028.2	70,466.8	25,123.3	60,763.8	7,178.6	35,942.1	1,169.0
Loblolly pine	4,653,085.0	291,563.8	340,022.2	64,006.6	3,899,543.3	412,198.5	280,556.4	26,514.3
Other yellow pines	675,399.5	23,452.9	32,172.5	16,132.5	31,720.3	4,577.7	13,682.1	891.0
Eastern hemlock	8,753.3	333.1	0.0	138.7	2,095.6	511.5	0.0	142.1
Cypress	220,895.2	6,866.7	533.3	468.6	237.9	0.0	0.0	0.0
Other softwoods	108,041.9	4,364.4	1,913.9	1,098.1	2,690.7	407.0	637.9	91.2
Total softwood	8,316,661.1	424,440.6	519,075.2	121,485.9	4,366,539.2	459,580.6	371,248.0	32,879.7
Hardwood								
Select white oaks	1,349,555.5	52,057.7	29,185.5	5,616.5	19,426.4	2,954.1	7,583.2	139.6
Select red oaks	600,700.9	15,623.9	9,661.8	5,738.9	4,157.3	749.1	2,721.4	340.1
Other white oaks	1,010,110.0	38,280.1	21,679.5	4,580.3	7,506.9	2,110.3	8,440.1	518.5
Other red oaks	3,366,462.0	137,374.9	82,852.9	35,771.0	92,341.3	13,046.0	32,916.2	2,636.8
Hickory	1,260,677.1	34,255.2	22,784.8	9,835.7	18,965.4	1,217.0	6,870.2	669.8
Hard maple	63,360.4	2,300.2	582.7	76.4	353.0	-208.0	109.4	257.3
Soft maple	341,994.8	14,857.8	6,214.7	2,453.3	5,700.6	828.0	1,556.1	565.3
Beech	150,075.4	4,144.5	727.8	418.7	635.8	268.0	594.1	0.0
Sweetgum	2,276,883.2	93,924.2	60,172.1	15,977.6	110,558.0	10,617.5	20,112.0	1,339.4
Tupelo-blackgum	1,216,068.6	29,743.6	16,789.0	6,723.0	7,557.5	454.0	2,918.0	410.7
Ash	349,280.1	14,171.7	4,202.0	3,073.5	6,310.5	949.0	1,159.0	0.0
Cottonwood	29,367.0	589.0	0.0	423.8	356.0	0.0	0.0	0.0
Basswood	52,471.1	2,505.6	533.3	796.7	682.7	136.0	0.0	0.0
Yellow-poplar	1,370,652.4	66,010.5	30,898.0	6,236.3	63,404.3	8,809.0	7,845.6	93.8
Black walnut	10,771.8	581.0	0.0	0.0	171.8	0.0	0.0	0.0
Other hardwoods	1,339,518.7	45,198.3	22,821.5	16,732.2	38,206.6	2,809.1	4,919.9	440.1
Total hardwood	14,787,948.9	551,618.3	309,105.6	114,453.9	376,334.1	44,739.1	97,745.2	7,411.5
All species	23,104,610.0	976,058.9	828,180.7	235,939.8	4,742,873.3	504,319.7	468,993.2	40,291.1

Numbers in columns may not sum to totals due to rounding.

0.0 = a value of > 0.0 and < 0.05 for the cell.

in natural stands and in planted stands differ considerably. Figure 36 illustrates the average number of live trees per acre, by diameter class, for both planted and natural stands. The average planted stand has more trees per acre in the 6- and 8-inch diameter classes than natural stands, but fewer in the larger diameter classes. In fact, natural stands have over twice as many trees per acre in the 12-inch class

and almost 5 times more in the 14-inch class. The average planted stand contains only 1 tree per acre that is 16 inches d.b.h., and < 1 tree per acre that is > 18 inches d.b.h. Natural stands have at least 2 trees per acre in each diameter class up to 20 and at least 2 trees per acre that are ≥ 22 inches d.b.h. (fig. 36).

(A) Diameter classes 2 to 6 inches

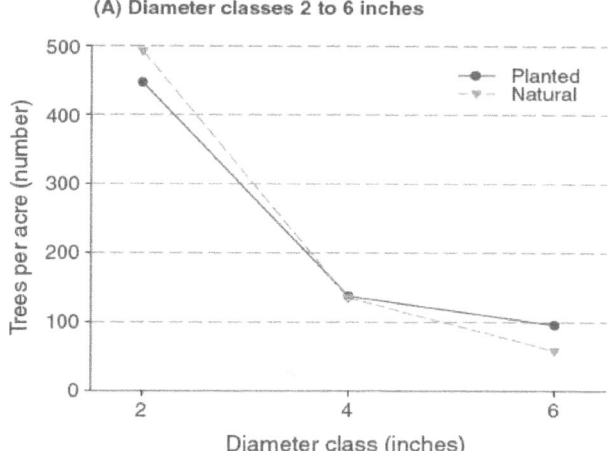

(B) Diameter classes ≥8 inches

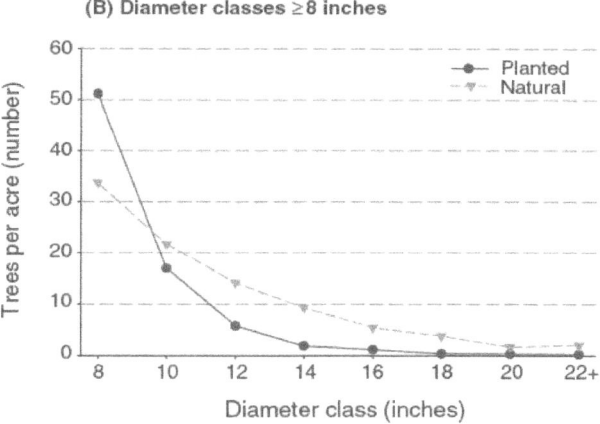

Figure 36—Average number of live trees per acre of timberland by diameter class and stand origin (A) 2- to 6-inches diameter classes, and (B) ≥8-inches diameter class, Alabama, 2000.

A barred owl in a tree. (photo by Ricky Layson, Ricky Layson Photography, Bugwood.org)

Differences in natural stands and planted stands become more obvious when similar comparisons are made based on softwood and hardwood delineations. Natural stands contain more hardwoods per acre in every diameter class, particularly in the larger diameter classes (fig. 37). Natural stands, on average, contain 5 times more hardwoods per acre in the 8-inch category, and up to 18 times the number of trees in the 18-inch diameter class. The average planted stand contains almost no hardwood trees > 14 inches d.b.h., while natural stands have at least 2 hardwoods per acre in every diameter class up to 18 inches and at least 2 trees per acre that are > 18 inches.

(A) Diameter classes 2 to 6 inches

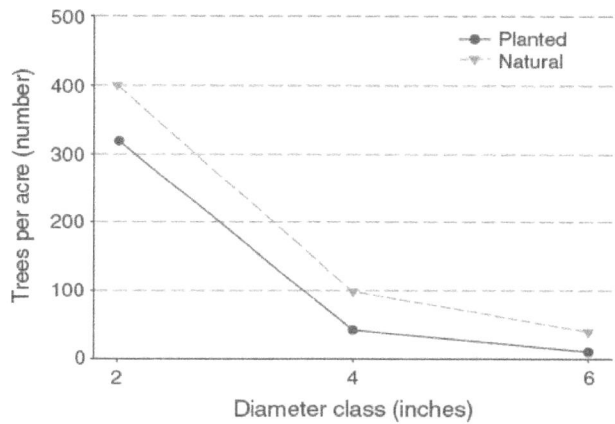

(B) Diameter classes ≥8 inches

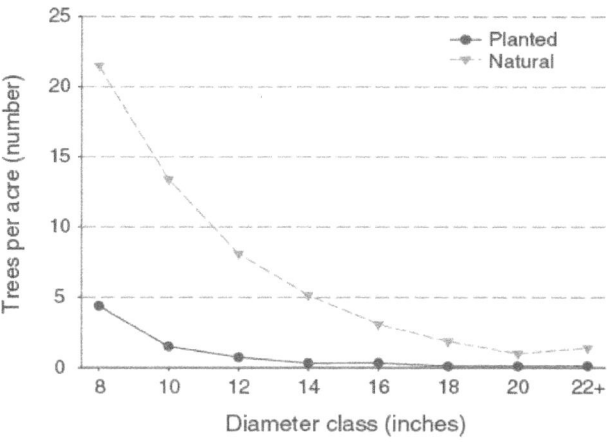

Figure 37—Average number of hardwood trees per acre of timberland by diameter class and stand origin (A) 2- to 6-inches diameter classes, and (B) ≥8-inches diameter classes, Alabama, 2000.

Figure 38 shows the average planted stand is composed primarily of smaller diameter softwoods, particularly those < 12 inches d.b.h. The average planted stand contains < 1 softwood per acre that is ≥ 16 inches d.b.h. Natural stands contain at least 2 softwoods per acre in each class up to 18 inches.

Generally, plantations are composed primarily of softwoods, particularly loblolly pine. Plantations produce more all-live volume than natural stands relative to standing volume. Natural stands tend to have a greater variety of species, especially hardwoods, and have larger diameter distributions.

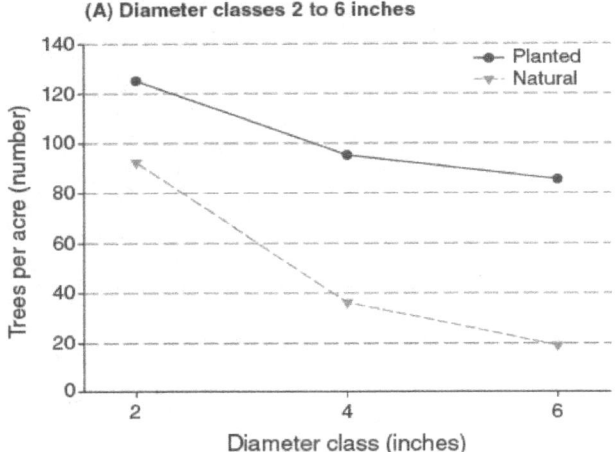

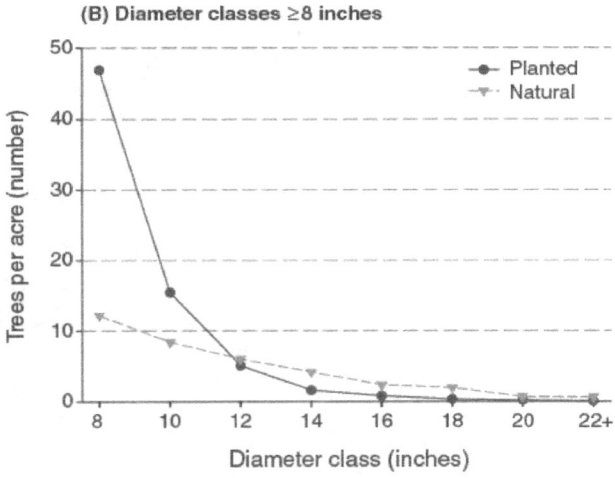

Figure 38—Average number of softwood trees per acre of timberland by diameter class and stand origin (A) 2- to 6-inches diameter classes, and (B) ≥8-inches diameter classes, Alabama, 2000.

Literature Cited

Abt, K.L.; Winter, S.A.; Wuggestt, R.J., Jr. 2002. Local economic impacts of forests. In: Wear, D.N.; Greis, J.G., eds. Southern forest resource assessment. Gen. Tech. Rep. SRS–53. Asheville, NC: U.S. Department of Agriculture Forest Service, Southern Research Station: 239–267.

Alabama Forestry Commission. 2002. Forest resource report for 2002. Montgomery, AL: Alabama Forestry Commission. 34 p.

Beers, T.W.; Miller, C.I. 1964. Point sampling: research results, theory, and applications. Resour. Bull. 786. Lafayette, IN: Purdue University Agriculture Experiment Station. 55 p. + insert.

Chamberlain, J.L.; Predny, M. 2003. Non-timber forest products enterprises in the South: perceived distribution and implications for sustainable forest management. In: Miller, J.E.; Midtbo, J.M., eds. Proceedings, first national symposium on sustainable natural resource-based alternative enterprises. Mississippi State, MS: Mississippi State University Extension Service and Mississippi State University, Forest and Wildlife Research Center: 48–63.

Hodgkins, E.J.; Cannon, T.L.; Miller, W.F. 1976. Forest habitat regions from satellite imagery: States of Alabama and Mississippi. [Map]. Supplement to Southern Cooperative Series Bull. 210. Auburn, AL: Alabama Agricultural Experiment Station; Mississippi State, MS: Mississippi Agriculture and Forestry Experiment Station.

Howell, M.; Gober, J.R.; Nix, J.S. 2002. Alabama's timber industry—an assessment of timber product output and use, 1999. Resour. Bull. SRS–75. Asheville, NC: U.S. Department of Agriculture Forest Service, Southern Research Station. 39 p.

Little, E.L., Jr. 1979. Checklist of United States trees (native and naturalized). Agric. Handb. 541. Washington, DC: U.S. Department of Agriculture. 375 p.

McWilliams, W.H. 1992. Forest resources of Alabama. Resour. Bull. SO–170. New Orleans: U.S. Department of Agriculture Forest Service, Southern Forest Experiment Station. 71 p.

Smith, W.B.; Miles, P.D.; Vissage, J.S.; Pugh, S.A. 2004. Forest resources of the United States, 2002. Gen. Tech. Rep. NC–241. St. Paul, MN: U.S. Department of Agriculture Forest Service, North Central Research Station. 137 p.

Sternitzke, H.S. 1963. Alabama forests. Resour. Bull. SO–3. New Orleans: U.S. Department of Agriculture Forest Service, Southern Forest Experiment Station. 32 p.

U.S. Department of Agriculture Forest Service. 1992. Forest Service resource inventories: an overview. Washington, DC: U.S. Department of Agriculture Forest Service. 39 p.

Van Deusen, P.C.; Dell, T.R.; Thomas, C.E. 1986. Volume growth estimation from permanent horizontal points. Forest Science: 32(2): 415–422.

Wheeler, P.R. 1953. Forest statistics for Alabama. For. Sur. Rel. No. 73. New Orleans: U.S. Department of Agriculture Forest Service, Southern Forest Experiment Station. 52 p.

Zahner, R. 1984. The soils and climate of the loblolly pine ecosystem, west region. In: Proceedings of the symposium on the loblolly pine ecosystem (west region). Mississippi State, MS: Mississippi State University, Mississippi State Cooperative Extension Service: 17–32.

Appendix

Inventory Methods

The Forest Inventory and Analysis (FIA) unit of the Forest Service, U.S. Department of Agriculture, Southern Research Station (SRS-FIA), conducts continuing inventories of forest resources in thirteen Southern States (Alabama, Arkansas, Florida, Georgia, Kentucky, Louisiana, Mississippi, North Carolina, Oklahoma, South Carolina, Tennessee, Texas, and Virginia), as well as Puerto Rico and the Virgin Islands. It is a collaborative partnership with the Southern Group of State Foresters of these States; the Southern region National Forest System; and State and Private Forestry.

SRS-FIA's mission is to conduct a program of research to improve the understanding of Southern forest ecosystems through inventories and analyses of the status and trends in resource conditions, use, productivity, and sustainability; and to conduct research to provide improved technology for timely and accurate resource inventories. Systematic periodic forest inventories in the Nation began after the McSweeney-McNary Forest Research Act was passed in 1928. This law is the basis of national forest inventories in the United States. The SRS-FIA program is an integral part of the national inventory. The Forest and Rangeland Renewable Resources Research Act of 1978 replaced earlier legislation. This Act was amended by the Agriculture Research, Extension, and Education Reform Act of 1998 (Farm Bill). It authorized a national, continuous, comprehensive survey and analysis of all renewable forest resources. SRS-FIA is a component of this national survey and analysis.

Clean water is vital to the future health and productivity of Alabama's forest resources. (photo by Kelvin J. Daniels)

The 2000 forest survey of Alabama was the seventh for the State since inventory work was authorized. Other surveys were conducted in 1935-36, 1951-53, 1963, 1972, 1982, and 1990. Inventory methods and techniques changed over the years. These changes were radical when compared to the 1935 to 1962 survey. However, from 1962 to 1990 the changes were more evolutionary rather than revolutionary; the same sampling and processing scheme was used, but refinements brought about by technological advances and user demands were incorporated.

The 2000 survey brought profound changes in inventory design, collection methods, and processing procedures. These changes were produced by a host of factors, many of which will be detailed in the sections that follow. The results of this transformation were: a merger of FIA and the Forest Health Monitoring (FHM) Program; a sample design that brought about national consistency among all FIA units; and development of a base from which annual inventories could subsequently be performed.

The following is a general description of the sample design and methods used to derive forest resource estimates provided in this report. Also, included is a brief discussion of past inventory design and methods to alert users to the changes. These changes necessitate caution when making comparisons to previous forest resource estimates.

Sample Design

The 2000 forest inventory of Alabama was conducted using a 3-phase, fixed-plot design. Phase 1 (P1) produces estimates of forest/nonforest area based on photointerpretation of specific points, or "dots," systematically located on aerial photos or digital images.

During Phase 2 (P2), a series of 24-foot, fixed-radius ground sample locations are established, where tree measurements and other data are collected to derive estimates of forest area, wood volume, tree growth, removals, and mortality. For this survey, all P2 plots were visited between May 1997 and April 2001. In the future, all P2 plot measurements will be visited annually on 20 percent of the total sample locations. After 5 years, all plots will be visited and the cycle will be completed.

Phase 3 (P3) of the sample design is conducted on a subset (1/16th) of the P2 sample locations. P3 measurements are combined with P2 plot measurements to assess the overall health of the State's forested ecosystems. A detailed description of the design of the P3 sample locations is provided in the section titled "Phase 3 Plot Design."

2000–Survey Plot Design

Plot design of the 2000 survey used a fixed-plot cluster composed of four 24-foot radius (1/24 of an acre) subplots spaced 120 feet apart (fig. A.1). The cumulative sample area of the four subplots is 1/6-acre, while the "footprint" of the cluster is about 1 acre. Trees ≥5.0 inches in d.b.h. are measured on each subplot. Trees >1.0 but <5.0-inches d.b.h. and seedlings (<1.0-inch d.b.h.) are measured on a microplot (1/300 of an acre; 6 feet, 8-inch radius) on each of the four subplots (fig. A.2). The microplot is offset 12 feet at 90 degrees from the subplot center.

A unique feature of this plot design is in the mapping of different land-use and forest conditions that are found in the plot cluster. Because the plots are established without bias, i.e., systematically, but at a scale large enough to be considered random, there is a probability that the plot cluster will straddle more than one type of land use or forest condition. When this occurs, the field crew draws a boundary across the plot so that the different homogeneous units can be identified and isolated.

There are two steps in the mapping process. The first involves identifying forest and nonforest areas on the plot and establishing a boundary line on the plot if both are present. The second step is to identify homogeneous areas in the plot's forested portion based on six factors: forest type,

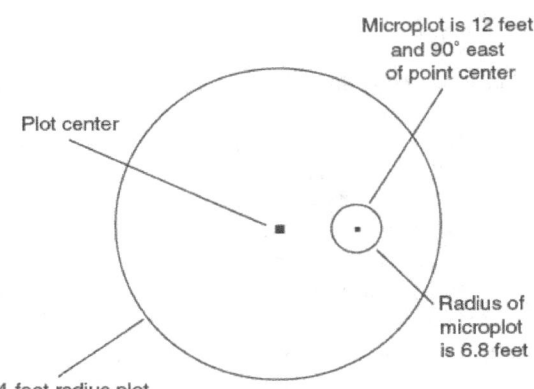

Figure A.2—Subplot layout.

stand size, ownership, stand density, regeneration status, and reserved status. These, too, are mapped into separate entities.

Previous Plot Design

All FIA inventories of Alabama between 1963 and 1990 used the same plot design, which was based on a variable radius or prism sampling technique. FIA field crews installed a sample plot cluster composed of 10 satellite points at each forested location. The cluster covered about 1 acre (fig. A.3). At each forested sample plot, trees ≥5.0-inches d.b.h. were selected with a 37.5 basal-area-factor prism at each of the 10 satellite points. Therefore, each tree selected with the prism represented 3.75 square feet of basal area. Trees <5.0- but >1.0-inches d.b.h. and seedlings (<1.0-inch d.b.h.) were tallied on a 1/275th acre circular fixed plot centered at the first 3 satellite points (fig. A.4).

There was no plot mapping done on the prism point cluster. Plot center (Point #1) was used to identify land use for the entire plot, either forest or nonforest. Points were moved or rotated into the forest condition if they happened to fall either inside of or <33 feet of a nonforest condition. If all 10 points were located on forest, they were left where they fell and were not rotated into homogeneous forest conditions if straddling more than one condition. Thus, data from multiple conditions was often collected and processed as if it were one continuous condition.

Phase 3 Plot Design

FIA collects data on forest health variables from a subset of P2 sample plots. The subset is about 1/16th of the P2 dataset, and is referred to as P3 of the forest inventory. Data collected on one P3 plot represents conditions on about 96,000 ground acres. Therefore, P3 data are coarse

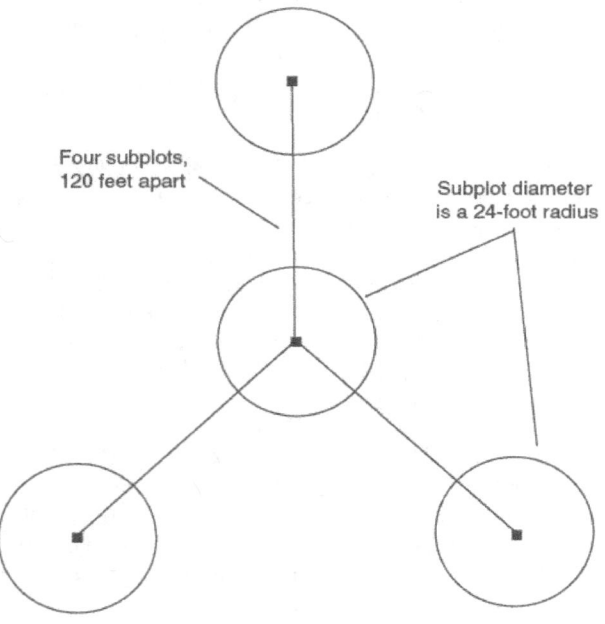

Figure A.1—Annual inventory fixed-plot design.

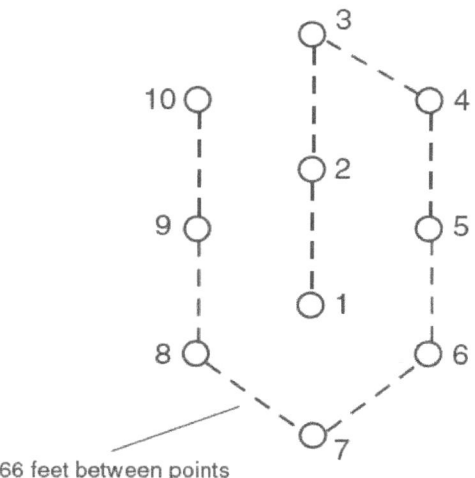

Figure A.3—Configuration of 10-point satellite sample unit.

66 feet between points

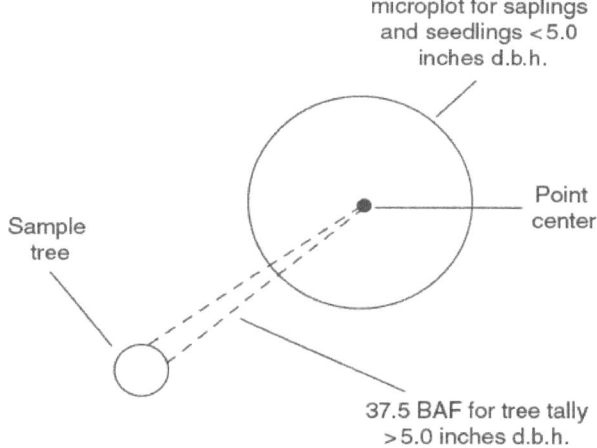

7.1 (6.8) foot radius microplot for saplings and seedlings <5.0 inches d.b.h.

Point center

Sample tree

37.5 BAF for tree tally >5.0 inches d.b.h.

Figure A.4—Configuration of one satellite point.

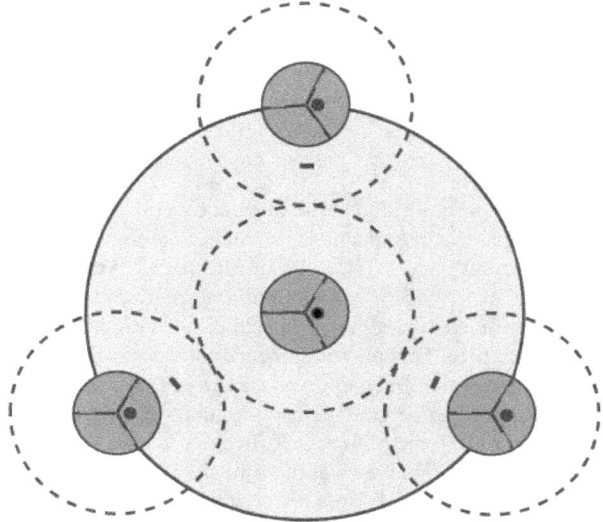

- Subplot—24.0 ft (7.32 m) radius
- Microplot—6.8 ft (2.07 m) radius
- Annular plot—58.9 ft (17.95 m) radius
- Lichens plot—120.0 ft (36.60 m) radius
- Vegetation plot—10.8 ft² (1.0 m²) area
- Soil sampling—(point sample)
- Down woody material—24 ft (7.32 m) subplot transects

Figure A.5—Layout of fixed-radius P2 and P3 plots used in Alabama survey.

descriptions and are meant to be used as general indicators of overall forest health over a large geographic area. Analyses of P3 data should not be done at levels below multiple-county aggregates.

P3 data collection includes variables pertaining to tree crown health, down woody material, ozone damage, lichen diversity, soil composition, and in some regions, nonwoody understory vegetation and diversity. Tree crown health, down woody material, soil composition, and nonwoody understory vegetation and diversity measurements are collected using the P2 plot structure, but lichen data are collected within a 120-foot radius circle the center of which is on subplot 1 of each FIA P3 field plot (fig. A.5).

Ozone data are collected independently of the FIA base grid because there are specific needs associated with ozone biomonitoring. Biomonitoring sites are selected based on specific criteria. Sites must be fields of about 1 acre or similar open areas adjacent to or surrounded by forest land, and must contain a minimum number of plants of which at least two are identified bioindicator species. Plants are evaluated for ozone injury, and voucher specimens are submitted to a regional expert for verification of ozone damage.

P3 data are collected on a temporally uniform schedule along with P2 plots. Ideally, 20 percent of P3 plots are collected annually (one "panel"), and a data cycle is complete in 5 years. Five years of P3 data present the most accurate statistical representation of surveyed forest land. In 2000, most States had <5 years worth of continuously collected forest health data on permanent P3 plots, so reporting has been restricted to data available at the survey's completion. In some cases, restricted sample sizes may result in the exclusion of a variable from analysis until a complete cycle of data collection has been made. Future reports will incorporate the full suite of P3 plots.

Additional details related to P3 of the FIA program, including field data collection manuals, can be found by following the "FIA Library" link from our Website at http://fia.fs.fed.us/.

Area Statistics

Sample sites were located at the intersection of lines on a 3-mile-square grid laid across the State. Theoretically, each plot represented 5,760 acres of forest land. Area estimation, or P1, was based on photointerpreting the ground use on each plot, as well as 25 photo sample points around each plot. This photointerpretation was performed by office personnel. Each dot was classified either as forest or nonforest, and a percentage for each class was derived for each county in the State. The office classifications were then checked by field crews at the time the plot was inventoried. Two correction factors are created by comparing forest/nonforest classifications identified by aerial imagery to the classification of that same point made on the ground. These correction factors are used to adjust the percent forest derived from the original estimate. The two correction factors adjust data from imaging (aerial photos) for possible misinterpretation of aerial photos and for changes that have occurred on the site since digital imagery was made. Formulas for the correction factors and the adjusted percent forest, which is the published value, are:

$CF1$ = # plots correctly PI'd forest/Total # of plots PI'd forest

$CF2$ = # plots PI'd nonforest but actually forest/Total # plots PI's nonforest

Percent Forest = (# forested dots * $CF1$) + (# nonforest dot counts * $CF2$)/Total dot count

Helping to manage the State's wildlife is often as easy as building bird boxes. (photo courtesy of the Alabama Forestry Commission)

During the 1970s, sampling intensity was increased by overlaying a 6-mile grid on the 3-mile grid. The plot centers and 25 associated sample points of these plots were photo-interpreted and verified by the field crews. No additional information was gathered from these locations. Rather, the information was applied to area-estimation procedures. These plots were referred to as "supplemental" plots, whose sole purpose was to strengthen the area estimation sample. Users may find reassuring the fact that except for the addition of "supplemental" plots, P1 methodology used in Alabama has not changed in over 50 years.

National forest land and reserved lands in a county were enumerated, i.e., acreages were taken from national forest reporting of their jurisdiction area. Ground sample locations were established on national forest lands and acreage representation, or the expansion factor on each plot, was a proportion of the known forest area in individual counties. This known area was then removed from the total county census area and the expansion factor for other forest land ownerships is based on the remaining acreage and associated plots.

Determining Stocking, Forest Type, and Stand Size

FIA used new procedures for assigning forest type and stand size classes to each condition observed on a plot. The procedures, definitions, and associated algorithms are designed by FIA nationally to provide consistency among States. The list of recognized forest types, grouping of these forest types for reporting purposes, models used to assign stocking values to individual trees, and names given to the forest types have changed. For conditions that were too small to have sufficient stocking for the algorithms (i.e., most mapped subplots), the field person assigned a forest type and stand size based on similar conditions outside the plot boundary. In all other cases, these classifications were derived using standard FIA procedures.

Stocking

At the individual tree level, stocking is the density value assigned to a sampled tree expressed as a percent of the total tree density required to fully utilize the growth potential of the land. At the stand level, stocking refers to the sum of the density value of all trees sampled.

Stocking is the basis for calculating stand size and forest type. Procedures used to assign stocking to individual trees differ with the change in survey design. Following is a brief summary of recent past and current methods used to calculate stocking, as well as to estimate forest type and stand size.

2000–Survey Stocking Methods

Stand size and forest-type classifications for each sample plot are based on a computation of stocking, based on tallied trees by forest condition (see Glossary). Samples include all forest conditions that fall within four 24-foot-radius circular plots (see Sample Design). Recorded observations include a seedling (<1.0-inch d.b.h.) count, a tally of all live trees 1.0 to 4.9 inches d.b.h. on a 6.8-foot-radius microplot, and a tally of all live trees 5.0-inches d.b.h. and larger for each 24-foot-radius plot.

Previous Stocking Methods

Surveys in the South conducted from the 1970s to the 1990s, based forest-type and stand-size classifications on a computation of stocking of tallied trees from a maximum of 10 sample points per forest land location (see Sample Design). Trees 1.0 to 4.9 inches d.b.h. were tallied on a 6.8-foot radius microplot. Trees 5.0 inches d.b.h. and larger were selected with a 37.5 basal area factor prism sample (proportional to size). Seedlings (<1.0 inch d.b.h.) were tallied only if no larger trees were present.

Forest Type

Forest type is based on and named for the tree species that form the plurality of live-tree stocking, and are at least 10 percent stocked with live trees. Forest type indicates the predominant live-tree species cover. Hardwoods and softwoods are first aggregated to determine the predominant group, and forest type is thereby selected. Eastern softwood groups have ≥50 percent softwood stocking and contain the named species that constitute a plurality of the stocking; the

White pine and shortleaf pine can be found in north Alabama. (photo by Andrew J. Hartsell)

oak-pine group has between 25 and 49 percent softwood; while the hardwood groups have <25 percent of their total all-live stocking in softwood species. The nonstocked group includes stands <10 percent stocked with live trees.

Under the variable radius sample design, a single forest type represented the entire location. The design used in 2000, a fixed-radius inventory design, identifies forest type for each forest condition. Thus prior surveys had greater numbers of "mixed" stands which, when inventoried for this survey, actually showed two or more conditions composed of distinct forest types. The methodology and formulas used to determine forest type were changed in an attempt to accommodate the evolution from variable radius sampling to fixed plot sampling.

Stand Size

Stand size is a computed classification of forest land based on the diameter class distribution of live trees in the stand. Under the variable radius sample design, a single stand-size class is determined and represents an entire location. The 2000's fixed-radius inventory design describes a stand size for each condition.

For the purposes of this report, stand-size class and forest type are based on both field calls and algorithms, depending on the existence of more than one condition on a plot. Plots with multiple conditions often used the field observation, while homogenous plots were derived from the algorithms. When updated, the national forest-type algorithm will be used to compute forest-type classifications.

Tree Volume

2000–Survey Volume Methods

Tree volumes were computed using a simple linear regression model (D^2H) that predicts gross cubic foot volume inside bark from a 1-foot stump to a 4-inch upper diameter outside bark for each sample tree based on diameter at breast height (D) and total height (H). Separate equation coefficients for 77 species or species groups were used. Volume in forks or limbs outside of the main bole was excluded. Net cubic foot volume was derived by subtracting a field crew estimate of rotten or missing wood for each sample tree. Volume of the saw-log portion (expressed in International 1/4-inch board feet and in cubic feet) of sample trees was computed using board foot-cubic foot ratio equations. All equations and coefficients were developed from standing and felled tree volume studies conducted across several Southern States.

Previous Methods

Methods for estimating tree volumes in the 1972 to 1990 inventories differed from those described above. Tree volumes were derived from several measurements on each tree tallied on forested sample plots. These measurements included d.b.h., bark thickness, total height, bole length, log length, and up to four upper-stem diameters that defined pole top, pole mid, saw top, and saw mid. Gross tree volumes (cubic and board foot values) were determined by applying the formula for a conic frustum to different sections of the bole. Each section's volume was then added to produce total stem volume. Net cubic foot volume was derived by subtracting a field crew estimate of rotten or missing wood for each sample tree. Earlier procedures also differed from current ones in that merchantable volumes were computed for the bole of trees from a 1-foot stump to an upper-stem stopping point determined by merchantability standards. The upper-stem diameter then could be as low as 4.0 inches but often was larger, depending on the perceived condition and merchantability of the upper tree bole.

Because of these differences in volume computation and merchantability standards, previously reported volumes may not be comparable to those reported in this inventory. To compare volumes, previous tree volumes were recomputed using the new equations. On average, recomputed values for tallied trees were higher than the original volumes for both softwood and hardwood species. Users should use caution when making rigorous comparisons between surveys due to the changes in volume computation methods and sample design.

A mallard duck takes flight. (photo by Erwin and Peggy Bauer, U.S. Fish and Wildlife Service, Bugwood.org)

Components of Change: Estimating Growth, Removals, and Mortality

One of the primary reasons for conducting forest inventories is to determine how much volume resides in southern forest stands, and to identify how and why it is changing. Survey-based estimates of tree growth, removals, and mortality provide some of the information needed to better understand resource change. The following is a discussion of current methods, i.e., those used to compile the 2000 report, and past methods used to derive resource estimates.

2000–Survey Methods

Estimates of volume change resulting from changes in growth, removals, and mortality, were determined from the remeasurement of sample plots established during the 1963 to 1990 inventories. The former plot design was based on a cluster of 10 "prism points" established at 66-foot, or 1-chain, intervals. At each prism point, trees 5.0 inches d.b.h. and larger were selected using a 37.5-basal-area-factor prism. Trees <5.0 inches d.b.h. but ≥1.0 inch d.b.h. were tallied on a 1/275-acre circular fixed plot centered at the first 3 prism points (see Sample Design).

During the 2000 remeasurement, some changes were made to the previous sample design. For trees <5.0 inches d.b.h. but ≥1.0 inch d.b.h., the 1/275-acre circular fixed plot on prism points 1 to 3 was reduced to a 1/300-acre circular fixed plot. For trees 5.0 inches d.b.h. and larger, only the first 5 of the 10 prism points were sampled, i.e., prism points one to five carry twice the weight they did in the previous inventory. These changes were made to achieve sampling consistency with the former Southeastern FIA unit.

For the Alabama 2000 survey, SRS-FIA used the Beers and Miller (1964) approach to determine growth, removal, and mortality estimates. This method was used to achieve efficiency in the field, requiring crews to account for previously tallied trees only, ignoring new ingrowth trees on the prism points. The only new tally trees on the prism points were those trees missed by the previous crew, or determined to be "through growth" on the 1/275-acre fixed circular plot on prism points 1 to 3. In addition, on reversions (previously nonforest land that has since reverted to forest land), all trees 5.0 inches d.b.h. or greater on the new subplot design located in the reverted forested condition were evaluated to determine if they qualify as remeasured 37.5-basal-area-factor tally trees (based on d.b.h. and distance).

A 25-year old pine plantation in Chambers County that has been pruned, prescribed burned, and thinned. (photo by David Stephens, Bugwood.org)

Previous Methods

The former Southern FIA unit estimated growth components using a Beers and Miller (1964) approach, as modified by Van Deusen and others (1986). The Van Deusen modification included new trees that grew into the prism sample. Every remeasured and new tree from all 10 points were used in computing components of change. Additionally, on reversions all trees 5.0 inches d.b.h. or greater on the new subplot design located in the reverted forested condition were evaluated to determine if they qualify as remeasured 37.5-basal-area-factor tally trees (based on d.b.h. and distance).

Comparing Data Among Surveys

Users wishing to make rigorous comparisons of data between or among surveys should be aware of significant differences in plot designs. The most valuable and powerful trend information comes from plots revisited from one survey to the next and measured in the same way. This is also the only method that yields reliable components of change estimation (growth, removals, and mortality). Although both designs may be judged statistically valid, the naturally occurring 'noise' in the data hinders confident and rigorous assessments of trends. When a design changes or plots are not remeasured, the true impact of such a change on trend analysis is unknown. The only way to quantify this impact with certainty would be to measure both plot designs simultaneously and compare the results of the two independent surveys. Neither the time nor money is available to do so.

Statistical Reliability

FIA inventories employ sampling methods designed to achieve reliable statistics at the survey unit and State levels. A measure of reliability of inventory statistics is provided by sampling errors. These sampling errors mean that the chances are two out of three that the true population value is within the limits indicated by the confidence interval. The following tabulation presents sampling errors (in percent) and associated confidence intervals around the sample estimates for timberland area, inventory volumes, and components of change.

Sampling error increases as the area or volume considered decreases in magnitude. Sampling errors and associated confidence intervals are often unacceptably high for small components of the total resource. Using the following formula, users can compute statistical confidence for any subdivision of the reported totals. Because this process assumes constant variance across all subdivisions of totals, sampling errors obtained by this method are only approximations.

$$SE_s = SE_t \left(\frac{\sqrt{X_t}}{X_s} \right)$$

where

SE_s = sampling error for subdivision of survey or unit total

SE_t = sampling error for survey unit or State total

The original forest on this site was cleared for a farm and later reverted back to forest. Now it is being converted to an urban subdivision. (photo by Andrew J. Hartsell)

X_s = sum of values for the variable of interest (area or volume) for subdivision of survey unit or State

X_t = total area or volume for survey unit or State

For example, the estimate of sampling error of hardwood growing-stock volume on NIPF land is computed as:

$$SE_s = 1.46 \ \frac{\sqrt{27,847.3}}{\sqrt{12,509.9}} = 2.18$$

Thus the sampling error is 2.18 percent, and the resulting confidence interval (two times out of three) for hardwood growing-stock volume on NIPF land is 12,509.9 ± 272.7 million cubic feet.

County statistics are provided, but users are cautioned that the accuracy of individual county data is highly variable. Individual county statistics are provided so that any combination of counties may be added together until the totals are large enough to meet the desired degree of reliability.

Item	Sample estimate and confidence interval		Sampling error
			percent
Timberland (1,000 acres)	22,925.8 ±	71.9	0.31
All live (million cubic feet)			
Inventory	31,125.9 ±	432.7	1.39
Net annual growth	1,613.5 ±	27.9	1.73
Annual removals	1,378.7 ±	40.9	2.97
Annual mortality	334.7 ±	10.9	3.25
Growing stock (million cubic feet)			
Inventory	27,847.3 ±	406.6	1.46
Net annual growth	1,480.3 ±	26.3	1.78
Annual removals	1,297.0 ±	38.9	3.00
Annual mortality	276.2 ±	9.8	3.56
Sawtimber (million board feet)			
Inventory	89,644.1 ±	1,837.7	2.05
Net annual growth	5,141.2 ±	101.8	1.98
Annual removals	4,256.5 ±	149.8	3.52
Annual mortality	888.9 ±	39.5	4.44

Species List[a]

Common name	Scientific name[b]	Common name	Scientific name[b]
Softwoods		**Hardwoods (continued)**	
Atlantic white-cedar	*Chamaecyparis thyoides* (L.) B.S.P.	American smoketree	*C. obovatus* Raf.
Southern redcedar	*Juniperus silicicola* (Small) Bailey	Hawthorn	*Crataegus* L.
Eastern redcedar	*J. virginiana* L.	Common persimmon	*Diospyros virginiana* L.
Sand pine	*Pinus clausa* (Chapm. ex Englem.) Vasey ex Sarg.	Russian-olive	*Elaeagnus angustifolia* L.
		American beech	*Fagus grandifolia* Ehrh.
Shortleaf pine	*P. echinata* Mill.	White ash	*Fraxinus americana* L.
Slash pine	*P. elliottii* Engelm.	Carolina ash	*F. caroliniana* Mill.
Spruce pine	*P. glabra* Walt.	Green ash	*F. pennsylvanica* Marsh.
Longleaf pine	*P. palustris* Mill.	Pumpkin ash	*F. profunda* (Bush) Bush
Pond pine	*P. serotina* Michx.	Blue ash	*F. quadrangulata* Michx.
Eastern white pine	*P. strobus* L.	Waterlocust	*Gleditsia aquatica* Marsh.
Loblolly pine	*P. taeda* L.	Honeylocust	*G. triacanthos* L.
Virginia pine	*P. virginiana* Mill.	Loblolly-bay	*Gordonia lasianthus* (L.) Ellis
Baldcypress	*Taxodium distichum* (L.) Rich.	Kentucky coffeetree	*Gymnocladus dioicus* (L.) K. Koch
Pondcypress	*T. distichum* var. *nutans* (Ait.) Sweet	Silverbell	*Halesia* Ellis ex L.
Eastern hemlock	*Tsuga canadensis* (L.) Carr.	American holly	*Ilex opaca* Ait. var. *opaca*
		Walnut	*Juglans* L.
Hardwoods		Butternut	*J. cinerea* L.
Florida maple	*Acer barbatum* Michx.	Black walnut	*J. nigra* L.
Chalk maple	*A. leucoderme* Small	Sweetgum	*Liquidambar styraciflua* L.
Boxelder	*A. negundo* L.	Yellow-poplar	*Liriodendron tulipifera* L.
Red maple	*A. rubrum* L.	Osage-orange	*Maclura pomifera* (Raf.) Schneid.
Silver maple	*A. saccharinum* L.	Cucumbertree	*Magnolia acuminata* L.
Sugar maple	*A. saccharum* Marsh.	Southern magnolia	*M. grandiflora* L.
Mountain maple	*A. spicatum* Lam.	Bigleaf magnolia	*M. macrophylla* Michx.
Ohio buckeye	*Aesculus glabra* Willd.	Sweetbay	*M. virginiana* L.
Yellow buckeye	*A. octandra* Marsh.	Apple	*Malus* spp. Mill.
Ailanthus	*Ailanthus altissima* (Mill.) Swingle	Chinaberry	*Melia azedarach* L.
Mimosa/silktree	*Albizia julibrissin* Durazzini	White mulberry	*Morus alba* L.
Serviceberry	*Amelanchier* Medic.	Red mulberry	*M. rubra* L.
Pawpaw	*Asimina triloba* (L.) Dunal	Water tupelo	*Nyssa aquatica* L.
Yellow birch	*Betula alleghaniensis* Britton	Ogeechee tupelo	*N. ogeche* Bartr. ex. Marsh.
Sweet birch	*B. lenta* L.	Blackgum	*N. sylvatica* Marsh.
River birch	*B. nigra* L.	Swamp tupelo	*N. sylvatica* var. *biflora* (Walt.) Sarg.
Gum bumelia	*Bumelia lanuginosa* (Michx.) Pers.	Eastern hophornbeam	*Ostrya virginiana* (Mill.) K. Koch
American hornbeam	*Carpinus caroliniana* Walt.	Sourwood	*Oxydendrum arboreum* (L.) DC.
Hickory	*Carya* spp. Nutt.	Royal paulownia	*Paulownia tomentosa* (Thunb.) Sieb. & Zucc. ex. Steud.
Water hickory	*C. aquatica* (Michx. f.) Nutt.		
Bitternut hickory	*C. cordiformis* (Wangenh.) K. Koch	Redbay	*Persea borbonia* (L.) Spreng.
Pignut hickory	*C. glabra* (Mill.) Sweet	Water-elm	*Planera aquatica* J.F. Gmel.
Pecan	*C. illinoensis* (Wangenh.) K. Koch	Sycamore	*Platanus occidentalis* L.
Shellbark hickory	*C. laciniosa* (Michx. f.) Loud.	Eastern cottonwood	*Populus deltoides* Bartr. ex Marsh.
Nutmeg hickory	*C. myristiciformis* (Michx. f.) Nutt.	Swamp cottonwood	*P. heterophylla* L.
Shagbark hickory	*C. ovata* (Mill.) K. Koch	Pin cherry	*Prunus pensylvanica* L. f.
Sand hickory	*C. pallida* (Ashe) Engl. & Graebn.	Black cherry	*P. serotina* Ehrh.
Black hickory	*C. texana* Buckl.	Chokecherry	*P. virginiana* L.
Mockernut hickory	*C. tomentosa* (Poir.) Nutt.	White oak	*Quercus alba* L.
American chestnut	*Castanea dentata* (Marsh.) Borkh.	Swamp white oak	*Q. bicolor* Willd.
Allegheny chinkapin	*C. pumila* Mill.	Scarlet oak	*Q. coccinea* Muenchh.
Southern catalpa	*Catalpa bignonioides* Walt.	Durand oak	*Q. durandii* Buckl.
Sugarberry	*Celtis laevigata* Willd.	Southern red oak	*Q. falcata* Michx.
Hackberry	*C. occidentalis* L.	Cherrybark oak	*Q. falcata* var. *pagodifolia* Ell.
Eastern redbud	*Cercis canadensis* L.	Bluejack oak	*Q. incana* Bartr.
Flowering dogwood	*Cornus florida* L.	Turkey oak	*Q. laevis* Walt.

continued

Species List[a] (continued)

Common name	Scientific name[b]	Common name	Scientific name[b]
Hardwoods (continued)		**Hardwoods (continued)**	
Laurel oak	*Q. laurifolia* Michx.	Delta post oak	*Q. stellata* var. *paludosa* Sarg.
Overcup oak	*Q. lyrata* Walt.	Black oak	*Q. velutina* Lam.
Blackjack oak	*Q. marilandica* Muenchh.	Live oak	*Q. virginiana* Mill.
Swamp chestnut oak	*Q. michauxii* Nutt.	Black locust	*Robinia pseudoacacia* L.
Dwarf live oak	*Q. minima* (Sarg.) Small	Black willow	*Salix nigra* Marsh.
Chinkapin oak	*Q. muehlenbergii* Engelm.	Chinese tallowtree	*Sapium sebiferum* (L.) Roxb.
Water oak	*Q. nigra* L.	Sassafras	*Sassafras albidum* (Nutt.) Nees
Nuttall oak	*Q. nuttallii* Palmer	American basswood	*Tilia americana* L.
Pin oak	*Q. palustris* Muenchh.	Carolina basswood	*T. caroliniana* Mill.
Willow oak	*Q. phellos* L.	White basswood	*T. heterophylla* Vent.
Chestnut oak	*Q. prinus* L.	Winged elm	*Ulmus alata* Michx.
Northern red oak	*Q. rubra* L.	American elm	*U. americana* L.
Shumard oak	*Q. shumardii* Buckl.	Siberian elm	*U. pumila* L.
Post oak	*Q. stellata* Wangenh.	Slippery elm	*U. rubra* Muhl.
Dwarf post oak	*Q. stellata* var. *margaretta* (Ashe) Sarg.	September elm	*U. serotina* Sarg.

[a] Common and scientific names of tree species ≥ 1.0 inch in d.b.h. occurring in the FIA sample.
[b] Little (1979).

Hardwood stands comprise almost one-half of Alabama's forest lands. (photo by Kelvin J. Daniels)

Glossary

Afforestation. Area of land previously classified as nonforest that is converted to forest by planting trees or by natural reversion to forest.

Average annual mortality. Average annual volume of trees ≥5.0 inches d.b.h. that died from natural causes during the intersurvey period.

Average annual removals. Average annual volume of trees ≥5.0 inches d.b.h. removed from the inventory by harvesting, cultural operations (such as timber stand improvement), land clearing, or changes in land use during the intersurvey period.

Average net annual growth. Average annual net change in volume of trees ≥5.0 inches d.b.h. in the absence of cutting (gross growth minus mortality) during the intersurvey period.

Basal area. The area in square feet of the cross section at breast height of a single tree or of all the trees in a stand, usually expressed in square feet per acre.

Biomass. The aboveground fresh weight of solid wood and bark in live trees ≥1.0 inch d.b.h. from the ground to the tip of the tree. All foliage is excluded. The weight of wood and bark in lateral limbs, secondary limbs, and twigs under 0.5 inch in diameter at the point of occurrence on sapling-size trees is included but is excluded on poletimber and sawtimber-size trees.

Bole. That portion of a tree between a 1-foot stump and a 4-inch top d.o.b. in trees ≥5.0 inches d.b.h.

Census water. Streams, sloughs, estuaries, canals, and other moving bodies of water ≥200 feet wide, and lakes, reservoirs, ponds, and other permanent bodies of water ≥4.5 acres in area.

Commercial species. Tree species currently or potentially suitable for industrial wood products.

Composite panels. Roundwood products manufactured into chips, wafers, strands, flakes, shavings, or sawdust and then reconstituted into a variety of panel and engineered lumber products.

CRP. The Conservation Reserve Program, a major Federal afforestation program authorized by the 1985 Farm Bill.

D.b.h. Tree diameter in inches (outside bark) at breast height (4.5 feet aboveground).

Diameter class. A classification of trees based on tree d.b.h. Two-inch diameter classes are commonly used by Forest Inventory and Analysis, with the even inch as the approximate midpoint for a class. For example, the 6-inch class includes trees 5.0 through 6.9 inches d.b.h.

D.o.b. (diameter outside bark). Stem diameter including bark.

Down woody material. Woody pieces of trees and shrubs that have been uprooted (no longer supporting growth) or severed from their root system, not self-supporting, and are lying on the ground. Previously named down woody debris.

Forest land. Land at least 10 percent stocked by forest trees of any size, or formerly having had such tree cover, and not currently developed for nonforest use. The minimum area considered for classification is 1 acre. Forested strips must be at least 120 feet wide.

Forest management type. A classification of timberland based on forest type and stand origin.

Pine plantation. Stands that (1) have been artificially regenerated by planting or direct seeding, (2) are classed as a pine or other softwood forest type, and (3) have at least 10 percent stocking.

Natural pine. Stands that (1) have not been artificially regenerated, (2) are classed as a pine or other softwood forest type, and (3) have at least 10 percent stocking.

Oak-pine. Stands that have at least 10 percent stocking and classed as a forest type of oak-pine.

Upland hardwood. Stands that have at least 10 percent stocking and classed as an oak-hickory or maple-beech-birch forest type.

Lowland hardwood. Stands that have at least 10 percent stocking with a forest type of oak-gum-cypress, elm-ash-cottonwood, palm, or other tropical.

Nonstocked stands. Stands <10 percent stocked with live trees.

Forest type. A classification of forest land based on the species forming a plurality of live-tree stocking. Major eastern forest-type groups are:

White-red-jack pine. Forests in which eastern white pine, red pine, or jack pine, singly or in combination, constitute a plurality of the stocking. (Common associates include hemlock, birch, and maple.)

Spruce-fir. Forests in which spruce or true firs, singly or in combination, constitute a plurality of the stocking. (Common associates include maple, birch, and hemlock.)

Longleaf-slash pine. Forests in which longleaf or slash pine, singly or in combination, constitute a plurality of the stocking. (Common associates include oak, hickory, and gum.)

Loblolly-shortleaf pine. Forests in which loblolly pine, shortleaf pine, or other southern yellow pines, except longleaf or slash pine, singly or in combination, constitute a plurality of the stocking. (Common associates include oak, hickory, and gum.)

Oak-pine. Forests in which hardwoods (usually upland oaks) constitute a plurality of the stocking but in which pines account for 25 to 50 percent of the stocking. (Common associates include gum, hickory, and yellow-poplar.)

Oak-hickory. Forests in which upland oaks or hickory, singly or in combination, constitute a plurality of the stocking, except where pines account for 25 to 50 percent, in which case the stand would be classified oak-pine. (Common associates include yellow-poplar, elm, maple, and black walnut.)

Oak-gum-cypress. Bottomland forests in which tupelo, blackgum, sweetgum, oaks, or southern cypress, singly or in combination, constitute a plurality of the stocking, except where pines account for 25 to 50 percent, in which case the stand would be classified oak-pine. (Common associates include cottonwood, willow, ash, elm, hackberry, and maple.)

Elm-ash-cottonwood. Forests in which elm, ash, or cottonwood, singly or in combination, constitute a plurality of the stocking. (Common associates include willow, sycamore, beech, and maple.)

Maple-beech-birch. Forests in which maple, beech, or yellow birch, singly or in combination, constitute a plurality of the stocking. (Common associates include hemlock, elm, basswood, and white pine.)

Nonstocked stands. Stands <10 percent stocked with live trees.

Forested tract size. The area of forest within the contiguous tract containing each Forest Inventory and Analysis sample plot.

Fresh weight. Mass of tree component at time of cutting.

Fuelwood. Roundwood harvested to produce some form of energy, e.g., heat and steam, in residential, industrial, or institutional settings.

Gross growth. Annual increase in volume of trees ≥5.0 inches d.b.h. in the absence of cutting and mortality. (Gross growth includes survivor growth, ingrowth, growth on ingrowth, growth on removals before removal, and growth on mortality before death.)

Growing-stock trees. Living trees of commercial species classified as sawtimber, poletimber, saplings, and seedlings. Trees must contain at least one 12-foot or two 8-foot logs in the saw-log portion, currently or potentially (if too small to qualify), to be classed as growing stock. The log(s) must meet dimension and merchantability standards to qualify. Trees must also have, currently or potentially, one-third of the gross board-foot volume in sound wood.

Growing-stock volume. The cubic-foot volume of sound wood in growing-stock trees at least 5.0 inches d.b.h. from a 1-foot stump to a minimum 4.0-inch top d.o.b. of the central stem.

Hardwoods. Dicotyledonous trees, usually broadleaf and deciduous.

Soft hardwoods. Hardwood species with an average specific gravity of ≤0.50, such as gums, yellow-poplar, cottonwoods, red maple, basswoods, and willows.

Hard hardwoods. Hardwood species with an average specific gravity >0.50 such as oaks, hard maples, hickories, and beech.

Industrial wood. All roundwood products except fuelwood.

Land area. The area of dry land and land temporarily or partly covered by water, such as marshes, swamps, and river floodplains (omitting tidal flats below mean high tide), streams, sloughs, estuaries, and canals <200 feet wide, and lakes, reservoirs, and ponds <4.5 acres in area.

Live trees. All living trees. All size classes, all tree classes, and both commercial and noncommercial species are included.

Log grade. A classification of logs based on external characteristics indicating quality or value.

Logging residues. The unused merchantable portion of growing-stock trees cut or destroyed during logging operations.

Net annual change. Increase or decrease in volume of live trees at least 5.0 inches d.b.h. Net annual change is equal to net annual growth minus average annual removals.

Noncommercial species. Tree species of typically small size, poor form, or inferior quality that normally do not develop into trees suitable for industrial wood products.

Nonforest land. Land that has never supported forests and land formerly forested where timber production is precluded by development for other uses.

Nonstocked stands. Stands < 10 percent stocked with live trees.

Other forest land. Forest land other than timberland and productive reserved forest land. It includes available and reserved forest land which is incapable of producing annually 20 cubic feet per acre of industrial wood under natural conditions, because of adverse site conditions such as sterile soils, dry climate, poor drainage, high elevation, steepness, or rockiness.

Other removals. The growing-stock volume of trees removed from the inventory by cultural operations such as timber stand improvement, land clearing, and other changes in land use, resulting in the removal of the trees from timberland.

Ownership. The property owned by one ownership unit, including all parcels of land in the United States.

National forest land. Federal land that has been legally designated as national forests or purchase units, and other land under the administration of the Forest Service, including experimental areas and Bankhead-Jones Title III land.

Forest industry land. Land owned by companies or individuals operating primary wood-using plants.

Nonindustrial private forest (NIPF) land. Privately owned land excluding forest industry land.

Corporate. Owned by corporations, including incorporated farm ownerships.

Individual. All lands owned by individuals, including farm operators.

Other public. An ownership class that includes all public lands except national forests.

Miscellaneous Federal land. Federal land other than national forests.

State, county, and municipal land. Land owned by States, counties, and local public agencies or municipalities or land leased to these governmental units for ≥ 50 years.

Plant residues. Wood material generated in the production of timber products at primary manufacturing plants.

Coarse residues. Material, such as slabs, edgings, trim, veneer cores and ends, suitable for chipping.

Fine residues. Material, such as sawdust, shavings, and veneer chippings, not suitable for chipping.

Plant byproducts. Residues (coarse or fine) used in the manufacture of industrial products for consumer use, or as fuel.

Unused plant residues. Residues (coarse or fine) not used for any product, including fuel.

Poletimber-size trees. Softwoods 5.0 to 8.9 inches d.b.h. and hardwoods 5.0 to 10.9 inches d.b.h.

Primary wood-using plants. Industries receiving round-wood or chips from roundwood for the manufacture of products, such as veneer, pulp, and lumber.

Productive-reserved forest land. Forest land sufficiently productive to qualify as timberland but withdrawn from timber utilization through statute or administrative regulation.

Pulpwood. A roundwood product that will be reduced to individual wood fibers by chemical or mechanical means. The fibers are used to make a broad generic group of pulp products that includes paper products, as well as fiberboard, insulating board, and paperboard.

Reforestation. Area of land previously classified as forest that is regenerated by planting trees or natural regeneration.

Rotten trees. Live trees of commercial species not containing at least one 12-foot saw log, or two noncontiguous saw logs, each 8 feet or longer, now or prospectively, primarily because of rot or missing sections, and with less than one-third of the gross board-foot tree volume in sound material.

Rough trees. Live trees of commercial species not containing at least one 12-foot saw log, or two noncontiguous saw logs, each 8 feet or longer, now or prospectively, primarily because of roughness, poor form, splits, and cracks, and with less than one-third of the gross board-foot tree volume in sound material; and live trees of noncommercial species.

Roundwood (roundwood logs). Logs, bolts, or other round sections cut from trees for industrial or consumer uses.

Roundwood chipped. Any timber cut primarily for pulpwood, delivered to nonpulpmills, chipped, and then sold to pulpmills as residues, including chipped tops, jump sections, whole trees, and pulpwood sticks.

Roundwood products. Any primary product such as lumber, poles, pilings, pulp, or fuelwood that is produced from roundwood.

Salvable dead trees. Standing or downed dead trees that were formerly growing stock and considered merchantable. Trees must be at least 5.0 inches d.b.h. to qualify.

Saplings. Live trees 1.0 to 5.0 inches d.b.h.

Saw log. A log meeting minimum standards of diameter, length, and defect, including logs at least 8 feet long, sound and straight, with a minimum diameter inside bark for softwoods of 6 inches (8 inches for hardwoods).

Saw-log portion. The part of the bole of sawtimber trees between a 1-foot stump and the saw-log top.

Saw-log top. The point on the bole of sawtimber trees above which a conventional saw log cannot be produced. The minimum saw-log top is 7.0 inches d.o.b. for softwoods and 9.0 inches d.o.b. for hardwoods.

Sawtimber-size trees. Softwoods ≥9.0 inches d.b.h. and hardwoods ≥11.0 inches d.b.h.

Sawtimber volume. Growing-stock volume in the saw-log portion of sawtimber-size trees in board feet (International 1/4 inch rule).

Seedlings. Trees <1.0 inch d.b.h. and >1 foot tall for hardwoods, >6 inches tall for softwood, and >0.5 inch in diameter at ground level for longleaf pine.

Select red oaks. A group of several red oak species composed of cherrybark, Shumard, and northern red oaks. Other red oak species are included in the "other red oaks" group.

Select white oaks. A group of several white oak species composed of white, swamp chestnut, swamp white, chinkapin, Durand, and bur oaks. Other white oak species are included in the "other white oaks" group.

Site class. A classification of forest land in terms of potential capacity to grow crops of industrial wood based on fully stocked natural stands.

Softwoods. Coniferous trees, usually evergreen, having leaves that are needles or scalelike.

Yellow pines. Loblolly, longleaf, slash, pond, shortleaf, pitch, Virginia, sand, spruce, and Table Mountain pines.

Other softwoods. Cypress, eastern redcedar, white-cedar, eastern white pine, eastern hemlock, spruce, and fir.

Stand age. The average age of dominant and codominant trees in the stand.

Stand origin. A classification of forest stands describing their means of origin.

Planted. Planted or artificially seeded.

Natural. No evidence of artificial regeneration.

Stand-size class. A classification of forest land based on the diameter class distribution of live trees in the stand.

Sawtimber stands. Stands at least 10 percent stocked with live trees, with one-half or more of total stocking in sawtimber and poletimber trees, and with sawtimber stocking at least equal to poletimber stocking.

Poletimber stands. Stands at least 10 percent stocked with live trees, of which one-half or more of total stocking is in poletimber and sawtimber trees, and with poletimber stocking exceeding that of sawtimber.

Sapling-seedling stands. Stands at least 10 percent stocked with live trees of which more than one-half of total stocking is saplings and seedlings.

Nonstocked stands. Stands <10 percent stocked with live trees.

Stocking. The degree of occupancy of land by trees, measured by basal area or the number of trees in a stand and spacing in the stand, compared with a minimum standard, depending on tree size, required to fully utilize the growth potential of the land.

Stocking categories are arbitrarily defined as follows:

Optimally stocked. Stands 61 to 100 percent stocked with growing-stock trees. Such stands are growing toward a fully stocked condition (the ideal space required for each tree increases with age). Optimum growth and bole form occur in this range.

Overstocked. Stands with >100 percent stocked with growing-stock trees. These stands become stagnant and mortality of individuals increases as stocking levels rise above 100 percent.

Understocked. Stands 0 to 60 percent stocked with growing-stock trees. Such stands will take a very long time to reach full stocking. Meanwhile, poor bole form will result, and much of the productive growth will occur on heavy limbs instead of on the bole.

Density of trees and basal area per acre required for full stocking

D.b.h. class	Trees per acre for full stocking	Basal area
inches		square feet per acre
Seedlings (< 1 inch)	600	—
2	560	—
4	460	—
6	340	67
8	240	84
10	155	85
12	115	90
14	90	96
16	72	101
18	60	106
20	51	111

— = not applicable.

Timberland. Forest land capable of producing 20 cubic feet of industrial wood per acre per year and not withdrawn from timber utilization.

Timber products. Roundwood products and byproducts.

Tree. Woody plants having one erect perennial stem or trunk at least 3 inches d.b.h., a more or less definitely formed crown of foliage, and a height of at least 13 feet (at maturity).

Tree grade. A classification of the saw-log portion of sawtimber trees based on: (1) the grade of the butt log or (2) the ability to produce at least one 12-foot or two 8-foot logs in the upper section of the saw-log portion. Tree grade is an indicator of quality; grade 1 is the best quality.

Upper-stem portion. The part of the main stem or fork of sawtimber trees above the saw-log top to minimum top diameter 4.0 inches outside bark or to the point where the main stem or fork breaks into limbs.

Veneer log. A roundwood product either rotary cut, sliced, stamped, or sawn into a variety of veneer products such as plywood, finished panels, veneer sheets, or sheathing.

Volume of live trees. The cubic-foot volume of sound wood in live trees at least 5.0 inches d.b.h. from a 1-foot stump to a minimum 4.0-inch top d.o.b. of the central stem.

Volume of saw-log portion of sawtimber trees. The cubic-foot volume of sound wood in the saw-log portion of sawtimber trees. Volume is the net result after deductions for rot, sweep, and other defects that affect use for lumber.

Metric Equivalents

1 acre = 4046.86 m^2 or 0.404686 ha
1 cubic foot = 0.028317 m^3
1 inch = 2.54 cm or 0.0254 m
Breast height = 1.4 m above the ground
1 square foot = 929.03 cm^2 or 0.0929 m^2
1 square foot per basal area per acre = 0.229568 m^2/ha
1 pound = 0.454 kg
1 ton = 0.907 MT